CAJUN CUISINE ™

Authentic Cajun Recipes From Louisiana's Bayou Country

Published by

Beau Bayou Publishing Company
Lafayette, Louisiana

DEDICATION

IN MEMORY OF MY FATHER, ROBERT J. ANGERS, JR.,

A world class journalist of the highest order, former President of the Louisiana Press Association and International Conference of Weekly Editors, who advised and counseled me in the production of this book. A fifty year career journalist in the heart of Louisiana's Cajun country, he wrote with love and devotion prolifically and incisively about Cajun subjects and his beloved Cajun country more than any man who has ever lived. Through his family, those he touched and inspired, the causes and issues he championed with vigor and integrity, the projects he influenced which read like a history of Louisiana in the 20th century, and through his abundant writings and his influence on his profession, his spirit, his wisdom, his vision, and his legend will live on forever.

W. Thomas Angers

TABLE OF CONTENTS

ACKNOWLEDGEMENTS

When we set out to produce *Cajun Cuisine* as a totally authentic Cajun cookbook, we did not know what an expansive project it would turn out to be. Fortunately, we were able to work with some of the best in all phases of the project, from recipe composition through final production.

We would first like to thank Sue Trosclair McDonough, who edited and screened the recipes. She is a graduate home economist and has spent her professional career in the Cajun Country in marketing for a major corporation and has operated a gourmet shop, taught cooking schools, managed a restaurant and worked for a Cajun catering service.

Special thanks go to our primary group of Cajun recipe contributors, including Leonard "Doc" Dauterive, Pat Gauthier Green and Harris Periou, all of Breaux Bridge, Louisiana, in St. Martin Parish; and M.A. "Mac" Greig of St. Martinville, also in St. Martin Parish. (St. Martin Parish, which is the setting for the conclusion of Longfellow's epic poem, "Evangeline," is the geographic heart and culinary epicenter of the fabulous Cajun food phenomenon.)

Others who contributed recipes include Mrs. Flossie Landry Purpera of Lafayette Parish, Mrs. Grace Broussard Veazey of Abbeville (Vermilion Parish), Mrs. Letha Savant Briggs of Lafayette Parish, Mrs. Dorothy Robichaux of Thibodaux (Lafourche Parish), Mrs. Verne Maraist Bienvenu, a native of St. Martin Parish, Mrs. Geraldine Beaullieu Angers, a native of Iberia Parish, and George E. Bulliard, Sr., Executive Vice-President and General Manager of Acadiana Pepper Company of St. Martinville, Louisiana.

Also contributing recipes and technical advice were Mrs. Marie Louise Comeaux Manuel, a resident of Lafayette Parish and former director of the School of Home Economics at the University of Southwestern Louisiana (USL); Mrs. Thelma Sonnier, former food service supervisor for Lafayette Parish; and Mrs. Elsie Castille, long-time Lafayette and St. Martin Parish Home Economist. These three ladies are among the nation's most knowledgeable on Cajun food.

Another contributor who also gave significant editorial advice was Miss C. Hazel Alpha, an outstanding Cajun home economist, who taught home economics in the Lafayette Parish school system for many years.

We would also like to thank Robert J. Angers Jr., who gave advice on most phases of this project. A working journalist in south Louisiana for nearly half a century, he is founder and currently *publisher emeritus* of *Acadiana Profile* magazine, which, since 1968, has dealt with the land, the people, events and customs of the 22-parish area of south Louisiana called Cajun Country, or "Acadiana."

Also we would like to thank Randy Herpin, who designed and produced *Cajun Cuisine*; Steve Angers, who assisted in these functions; and Glade Bilby II and his food stylist, Martha Torres, who designed and photographed the cover of the book.

FOREWORD

Beau Bayou Publishing Company, the publisher of *Cajun Cuisine*, was named after Beau Bayou, situated deep in the heart of Louisiana's Atchafalaya Basin where my great-great-great grandfather, Jean Baptiste Angers, first settled on land patented to him directly from the State of Louisiana. These lands, in turn, were acquired by the State of Louisiana under the Federal Swamplands Act whereby the State, by Congressional authority, selected and was granted certain lands deep in the heart of Louisiana's Cajun Country and granted them to the very early settlers of this region. Our family has been in Louisiana for over 165 years, all of that time residing in the heart of Cajun Country.

The cookbook which follows is a totally authentic Cajun cookbook, drawing on the experience and expertise of my family and the many experts given in the Acknowledgements section.

Cajun cuisine is a totally indigenous American cuisine, drawing from pure French, pure Spanish, Acadian and other Louisiana French elements as well as Black, Indian and other elements in Louisiana's history and culture and is a traditional food having evolved over a prolonged period of time. As discussed in the article which follows, Cajun cuisine is a cuisine which has drawn upon the foods native to Louisiana including Louisiana's abundant, high quality seafood, game, poultry, pork and beef. Contrary to what has been mistakenly reported elsewhere, Cajun cuisine is distinctive from Louisiana's Creole cuisine of New Orleans, although the two may have shared some similar influences. Nevertheless, as is discussed hereafter, Cajun and Creole cuisine are two distinct American styles of cooking.

The article which follows serves as an introduction to the extraordinary culinary phenomenon that we call Cajun cuisine. It was written by Mrs. Marie Louise Comeaux Manuel, a native Cajun and Director Emeritus of the School of Home Economics at the University of Southwestern Louisiana in Lafayette, Louisiana, also known as the "Cajun University" because it is situated in the heart of Cajun Country and serves the entire Cajun region of Louisiana, also known as Acadiana. Mrs. Manuel is the daughter of Alcin Thomas Comeaux and Louise Azema Doucet, both native Cajuns of the area. She is the world's foremost authority on the subject of Cajun cuisine, being both a descendant of Cajuns on her maternal and paternal side and having researched, written, studied and taught about Cajun cuisine throughout her career. No one knows more about this subject.

She holds a Bachelor of Science degree in Home Economics Education from the University of Southwestern Louisiana and a Master of Arts with a major in Foods and Nutrition from George Peabody College. She has also studied at Iowa State University, Cornell University, the University of Minnesota, New York University and the University of Wisconsin. In 1938, she assumed the position of head of the Home Economics Department at the University of Southwestern Louisiana and in 1951, when the department was changed to the School of Home Economics, Mrs. Manuel was named the director of the school. She remained in that position until 1970 when she retired. She has held positions in numerous professional organizations, including president of the Louisiana Home Economics Association, president of the Louisiana Vocational Association, secretary-treasurer of the Louisiana College Conference and secretary of the Acadiana Advisory Counsel on Aging. She was one of 200 American Home Economists Association members named to serve as French interpreters to the International Congress on Home Economics held at various times in Maryland, Paris, France and Bristol, England. She has received many honors and awards including the Pro Eacesia et Pontifice Medal awarded by the Pope, inclusion in American Magazine's list of "Interesting People" and membership in Phi Kappa Phi.

The following article, which serves as an introduction to the recipe manuscript, contains information on the origins and nature of Cajun cuisine, the major aspects of Cajun cuisine, some of the primary dishes, ingredients and procedures used in the preparation of Cajun cuisine, the distinction between Cajun and Creole cuisine as well as other information. This article is the most authoritative short treatise ever written on this subject.

W. Thomas Angers
President
Beau Bayou Publishing Company

6

ACADIAN (CAJUN) CUISINE

By MARIE LOUISE COMEAUX MANUEL
Director School of Home Economics (Retired)
University of Southwestern Louisiana

Good cooking is a subject of paramount interest to any healthy person and, because I am an Acadian, our cuisine holds for me not only an epicurean but also a sentimental historical appeal. We, the offspring, should take off our hats to the pioneer Acadian women and honor them with gratitude and admiration. Yes, we, a soft, pampered generation, owe a big debt to those women who made possible the existence of the Acadian Cuisine and the survival of the art. They brought with them something far more precious than the iron pots and pans: their culinary lore, a precious heritage from long generations of ancestors to whom cooking was the finest of arts. They faced the vast forested wilderness with composure, unsurpassed courage and creativeness.

The excellence of good cooking in south Louisiana dates back over two centuries. The French-Acadians brought to south Louisiana the tradition of *La Bonne Cuisine*, when they were banished from Nova Scotia by the British. They brought very few possessions. Consequently a great deal of thought, imagination and endless effort and work was necessary for their survival. Here they found a great variety of seafood, an overflowing supply of wild game, rich soil, ample water and semi-tropical weather. Adding to this natural wealth, they displayed their experiences, practical ability, firm belief, ingenuity and patience. They hoped to develop a cuisine which would be unsurpassed. In due time they became friendly with those of African, Spanish and Italian descent in this region. Through their association with these natives and their personal knowledge, the Acadians developed and perfected new recipes.

What is Acadian Cuisine? Stranger, be seated once at our distinguished board and you will become a lasting friend.

Acadian (Cajun) Cuisine is a recipe in itself. For ingredients take the classical French cuisine, combine it with Spanish classical cuisine, blend well, take herbs and spices from France and Spain and sometimes couple with seasoning learned from the Choctaws and Chickasaws. Then be sure to add the ingenuity, the creativity and the keen taste of refugee Acadians, who had to learn the use of nature's own food wherever these were to be found. Now, add the exotic taste and magic seasoning of the African cook. Voila! This is the Acadian cuisine whose tenets are economy and simplicity governed by patience and skill to produce a subtle, exotic and succulent cuisine.

This recipe for Acadian Cuisine may sound a great deal like Creole cuisine. You're right, it does, but please note there is a slight difference in the two cuisines. A Creole is a native of Louisiana born of European parentage. I maintain that we have Creole Cuisine — and Acadian Cuisine. The two have much similarity but also many differences. Through research, study and experience I found that:

Acadian Cuisine, unlike Creole Cuisine, uses herbs, seasoning and spices to bring out the full taste of the main ingredient. Thus, the product is not highly seasoned and the original flavor of the main ingredient predominates. There is a French saying, *"L'exces en tout est defaut"* (Excess is always a fault), which well describes Acadian Cuisine. A dish is a blend of ingredients which either "set off" or "tone down" to create a new and delicious taste. When an Acadian uses seasonings, spices or herbs, it is not because they are tasty; it is because these bring out the flavor of the meat, fish or whatever food she is preparing. Thereby, food becomes more delectable and unique in taste. If the flavor of any one of the seasonings, herbs or spices stands out, the dish is considered a failure.

Another difference in the Creole and Acadian Cuisine is that the Acadian dishes are not as greasy or there is not excess fat. The French leave a minimum of fat in a completed dish. When the recipe says "Pour fat off skillet," the Acadian cook does just that to "de-glace" the pan (i.e. to pour a little cold water in the skillet and scrape loose the browned part to add flavor and finesse to the dish), in other words, *une sauce rouille.* Because the Acadian homemaker was very economical, we find through her ingenuity, patience and a keen sense of taste, the third difference between Creole and Acadian cuisine, namely, those numerous, delicious, attractive wholesome dishes made from leftovers such as: stuffed vegetables, stews, puddings, soups, etc.

Food, its preparation and consumption, must be classified as Acadian pleasure. To my mother and my grandmothers, who were eyewitnesses of Acadian cookery, I have been greatly indebted for the many particulars of cooking which they related to me. They taught me that good eating is a fine art and we spent a good bit of our time practicing and enjoying it in a grand manner. They told me that in creating any improvisations of native food it is always best to mate fowl, fish and game with the fruits of the fields and woods that are currently in harvest, for all these edibles complement each other.

There are several requisite elements in Acadian cookery:

THE IRON POT: Because it retains heat and does not burn. Mother said, *"Qui va doucettement va surement"* (He who goes slowly goes surely).

THE ROUX: Typical of many Louisiana dishes is the inclusion of a roux, and the success of producing a delectable dish is to prepare a good roux. It is amazing how many tips may be given to cook two simple ingredients, flour and fat, so as to obtain a good product. Any good Acadian cook would say that the way to be successful in making a good roux is to sprinkle flour slowly in melted shortening, to brown it slowly and to stir continuously. Then, the secret is to gradually add cold water or stock, spices and herbs. My mother always said, "Add cold water to the roux. If hot water is added, the roux will be pale," meaning hot water bleaches the roux. (See page 213.)

STOCK: Game, meat, bones, fowl flesh, fish, all boiled together. From the time of the first cabin in this area, a stock pot had a prominent place on the south Louisiana stove. Game meat and bones, fowl flesh and bones, whole fish and the fish heads (the flavor and oils are in the head), crawfish and their shells, shrimp and their shells, crabs and the scrapings from the shells, and oyster juice are all boiled for stock. Vegetables and other items are added to the stock for soups and stews. Small amounts of stock are used in making gravies for the roasting pan, in basting and in almost all cooking.

HERBS AND SPICES: Although limited to the early Acadians they dared and imagined uses with these. Dried ones are twice as strong as the fresh. Each home had its herb garden planted between the smoke house and the big house. A few of the herbs grown were onions, parsley, celery, garlic, marjoram, chives, onion tops and bay leaves. Herbs and spices are obtained from the roots, stems, leaves, seeds or fruits of many plants. Some herbs may even have been brought here by the French and Spanish. Others are native to this area.

The nourishment of the Acadian families has through the centuries been very varied. Today the three meals of the day consist of the little breakfast, the dinner at noon (which is ordinarily the main meal of the day), and the supper. The little breakfast consists of a cereal, eggs, sausage, bread, butter, cane syrup, milk and coffee. The cereal may be grits or *couche-couche*. The bread may be cornbread, "lost bread," corn fritters or a variety of spoon breads. Twenty to thirty years ago *couche-couche* was commonly served in the Acadian homes with milk or with sausage and a rusty gravy or syrup. Corn fritters and syrup were more frequently served than today. Rice has always been present on the Acadian dinner table. In addition, the dinner menu consists of a meat or fish, Irish potatoes, sweet potatoes or corn, green vegetables, salad or marinated vegetables. The meat may be veal, beef, lamb, poultry, pork, turtle, frogs or wild birds. Fish of many kinds, crabs, shrimp, crawfish, trout and redfish form the main part of meals. The dessert may be preserved fruits, pie, cake or pudding. The night meal or supper frequently consists of an attractive dish or dishes prepared from the leftovers of the main meal. Sometimes syrup, cornbread, milk and milk products make up the last meal of the day. Milk, butter, clabber, cream cheese and cheese appear frequently on the tables.

Dishes which are typical of Acadian cuisine are many. Here are a few:

GUMBO: This dish would be termed a hearty, soupy stew. Conserving the wealth of one's findings has always been a trait of the Acadians. Upon their arrival in south Louisiana, they found an abundance and a variety of seafood. Being conservative and possessing a great deal of ingenuity, they concocted the delectable dish, gumbo. It was soon discovered that a gumbo could be prepared by the use of fowl, wild game, sausage, *andouille*, chitterlings and

9

"tasso" (a slim piece of smoked meat). Gumbo is prepared by starting with a roux. The roux is the heart of the gumbo. When the roux has reached its right consistency, the chopped onions, celery and green peppers are added. This mixture is cooked slowly until the onions are transparent and the green pepper and celery are soft. Cold water is then added slowly and to this mixture add one or a combination of the following: chicken, turkey, guinea, duck, geese, wild birds, rabbit, squirrel, veal, pork, sausage, crawfish, crab, shrimp or oysters. *Andouille* or "tasso" may be added to render a more tasty product.

The true Acadians seasoned and browned their meat before adding to it, resulting in a more tasty and colorful product. When the meat starts to recede from the bone, additional seasoning may be added and also the onion tops and parsley. *Filé*, a thickening agent prepared from crushed sassafras leaves, is added just prior to serving. Gumbo is served with rice, green salad, plain or garlic bread.

"Gumbo" is an African word, contrary to the best authority on Creole and Cajun cookery. It has long been thought to be French, perhaps because the French were quick to accept a good thing when they learn of it. In Africa, okra is called gumbo but gumbo is really a Portuguese corruption of *quin gombo*, which, in turn, is a corruption of *guillobo*, the native word for okra in the Congo and Angola area of Africa. Okra took quite a journey before arriving in America.

When the Negro was brought to America as a slave, he brought with him a variety of African things. When he boarded the slave ships he brought with him the seeds of his favorite foods. At least one of these seeds survived, in the West Indies and thence to the United States, with a native name "gumbo." It is the okra that exists all over Africa and has spread over the United States.

SOUP-EN-FAMILLE: The French trait of economy, as shown in the Acadians, is often called upon to balance an over-drawn budget, in which case *soup-en-famille* is cooked. This is a vegetable soup cooked with *bouille*, a beef brisket, which is served hot, garnished with the vegetables of the soup.

COURTBOUILLON is not commonly found other than in south Louisiana. The secret of this dish is in the blending of the fish (usually redfish), herbs, wine and water. They are at their best when cooked slowly right after the fish is caught. Many *courtbouillons* start with a roux.

CRAWFISH BISQUE is a soup full of crawfish "heads" stuffed with the meat of the tails.

ACADIAN JAMBALAYA is not a mixture of boiled rice and gravy made from giblets, herbs and seasonings. Boiled rice and gravy is rice dressing. Jambalaya is the completed product of the skillful blending of many flavors of which none predominates. It should be cooked in a big iron skillet. First, chop the onions and celery stalks, then add sweet pickled pork, ham or salt pork, foul or game. Add juice of oysters. Heat fat in another pot; cook onions slowly. Combine all, boil until tender. Add other meats, add water, bring to a boil. Then add rice and simmer until rice is tender. Lastly, add oysters. Oysters are cooked just long enough for edges to curl. Serve dotted with butter and sprinkled with parsley.

Reverend Robert Hamill Nassau stated in his article "Fetishism in West Africa" (published by Young Peoples Missionary Movement in 1904) that the most attractive native mode of cooking fish and meat is *Jomba* (bundle). The flesh is cut into pieces and laid in layers with salt, pepper, some crushed oily nut and a little water. All these are tied up tightly in several thicknesses of fresh green plantain leaves, and the bundle is set on a bed of hot coals. The water in the bundle is converted into steam before the thick fleshy leaves are charred through. The steam, unable to escape, permeates the fibers of the meat, thoroughly cooking it without boiling or burning.

From this I conclude that the Africans told the Acadian homemaker about the *Jomba*. The Acadians, through their skill in economizing, used rice instead of the crushed oily nuts of the Africans and named the product jambalaya.

TARTE A LA BOUILLIE: I can still remember my grandmother's *tarte a la bouillie*. She made a quick sweet rich dough and filled this pie with luscious rich vanilla custard. Hot or cold, it was delicious. This wonderful pudding pie is a traditional treat.

MAQUE CHOUX is a dish made of sweet corn, smothered with onions, fat, seasoning, garlic and one red tomato.

DAUBE GLACE is a jellied dish made with herbs, pig's feet and sometimes parts of the head and tongue.

RIZ AU LAIT is a dessert made of rice dolled in milk.

LACUITE is heavy cane syrup just before it turns to sugar. The late Mr. Wesley Steen of Abbeville, La., revived the making of *LaCuite*, and it is now sold commercially. Acadian Cuisine calls for chopping pecans very fine, then dipping a teaspoonful of *LaCuite* into the chopped pecans and serving it with hot coffee.

BOUILLABAISSE is a fish chowder made of two kinds of fish, usually redfish and red snapper, cooked with crabs, crawfish, shrimp, wine and appropriate seasoning.

PATE DE FOIE GRAS is made with goose liver in France. Acadian Cuisine, using the same method, developed a delectable *pate de foie gras* using calf or hog liver.

OREILLE DE COCHON or *PATE DE GROS BEC:* Louise Girard of Lafayette, Louisiana, is known for her *Oreille de Cochon*, but she refuses to give her recipe or allow anyone to see her preparing this delicacy. This is typical of many who are of African descent and of some of Acadian descent. Their reason is that they wish to leave their recipes and techniques to the younger members of their family. *Oreille de Cochon* is a dough mixture of flour, butter, egg, vinegar and salt, rolled out paper-thin, cut in squares (size of hand) and fried in deep fat, giving it a slight twist in the center with a fork while frying. Sprinkle while hot with powdered sugar or syrup, which has been boiled to the soft-ball stage. Delicious with coffee.

PRALINES AU BENE are pralines made with sesame seeds. *Praline au bene* served on corn shucks — Do you remember that wonderful taste? The corn shucks gave an aroma which can't be equaled. We do not see that anymore.

TAC-TAC: Christmas without popcorn balls was not Christmas in the Acadian homes of yesterday. Nor was a Christmas tree completely decorated unless it had strings of popcorn. That was yesterday, not today.

APPETIZERS: The Acadians say these little taste treats should be served only to whet one's appetite. Make them tasty and eye-appealing, but serve only a few.

SAUCES AND SUCH: Experienced French cooks know that the extra something that transforms plain food into earthly delight is a good sauce. It is *savoir faire* indeed if you use one of these: shallots, green pepper, grapefruit, apricot, wine, cheese and many others.

FISH: Louisiana's southern boundary and the Gulf of Mexico is the meeting place and home of some of the finest fish. The many bayous and the Gulf provided the ingredients for many tasty Acadian dishes too numerous to name here.

FOR DESSERT: Some exotic trifle, a choice of pies, custards, creams, cookies, cakes are fragments of tradition that will imbue the dinner with nostalgia in the days ahead. And then, a small *cafe noir*. This is the proper combination for *le coupe de grace de la cuisine Acadian*.

LA BOUCHERIE DE COMPAGNE or *LA BOUCHERIE DE SOCIETE* was an organization composed of twenty members of the neighborhood. *La Boucherie de Compagne* furnished meat to each member once every week, although each furnished a calf only once in twenty weeks. The hog butchering, or *la boucherie de cochon*, included sizzling of the crackling in the big open kettle, the hog-head cheese, the *griade a la marinea*, and *boudin blanc* and *boudin rouge*.

These industrious Acadians, with survival uppermost in their minds, took the wild birds from the air, the fish from the bayous and the Gulf, the grain, vegetables and fruit from the land, and accepted customs from the Indians, Spaniards and Africans, then concocted and handed down recipes that are enjoyed by most of us here and sometimes by others who have the good fortune to taste our cuisine. Acadian recipes are in great demand.

My aim through the years has been to teach the coming generation to enjoy meals which are exact replicas of our great grandmothers'. Acadian dishes were a part of the foods courses at the University of Southwestern Louisiana during the years 1935 to 1970, the years I directed the School of Home Economics. This took time, because my faculty members came from Texas, Oklahoma, Arkansas or Iowa. They had to learn how to prepare the Acadian dishes themselves before they could instruct their students. Today the graduates from these years include, in a limited amount, some of the Acadian dishes in their high school teachings. But there is still some hesitancy, since the textbooks do not include Acadian cookery.

Yes, the earlier Acadians were simple folk who loved life and the land where nature was exceptionally kind and where they prospered here in south Louisiana. Their ceremonies and festivals marking the blessings of their toils are nationally known. Such dishes as jambalaya, *courtbouillon*, rice, grits, *grillade*, *pain perdu*, *couche-couche caille* and gumbo have firmly established them on the culinary map.

When life itself was a gamble, they made their lives pay. They got out of the iron pot what they put in it — artistry, patience, simplicity, economy, skill and infinite finesse. We owe them a tribute — the survival of their art, the survival of the Acadian Cuisine.

GLOSSARY

ANDOUILLE: A popular reddish Cajun pork sausage made from pork stomach and other ingredients.

BISQUE: A popular Cajun soup often made with crawfish, in which the crawfish heads are stuffed with meat of the tails and placed in the soup bowl.

BOUCHERIE: A great Cajun tradition whereby groups of families got together once a week to butcher one or more calves or pigs, thereafter dividing the various cuts and making various Cajun dishes such as boudin, hogshead cheese, and cracklin from portions of the pigs.

BOUDIN: A popular Cajun pork sausage, usually light in color, made with various parts of pork and rice.

BOUILLABAISSE: A fish chowder made by layering fish and tomatoes and other seasonings in alternate layers and cooking in a heavy pot.

CAYENNE: A long, thin, red hot pepper frequently used as a seasoning in many Cajun dishes, more commonly available in ground form.

COURTBOUILLON: A Cajun fish soup made by first making a roux and including tomatoes and served with rice.

CRACKLINS: A dish made by frying small cut portions of pork skin and pork fat; also called "gratons."

CRAWFISH: A plentiful Louisiana crustacean used in many classic Cajun dishes which looks like a small lobster.

DAUBE GLACE: A jellied dish made with herbs and various parts of the pig or calf.

ETOUFFEE: A method of Cajun food preparation meaning smothered and cooked without a roux; used to cook crawfish, fish and other dishes.

FILE: Ground sassafras leaves used to add flavor and as a thickening agent in gumbos and other soups.

FRICASSEE: A Cajun stew made with a roux and chicken, duck, venison, beef or other meats and served over rice.

GREEN ONIONS: A very commonly used seasoning in Cajun dishes; also sometimes referred to as shallots by the Cajuns.

GUMBO: A soup or stew usually made with a roux and including meats commonly available in Cajun country, such as fowl, game, Cajun sausages and tasso.

JAMBALAYA: A Cajun dish in which pork, game and various other ingredients are cooked together with rice, as distinguished from a rice dressing which is a mixture of cooked rice and other ingredients such as cooked meats.

LAGNIAPPE: A French word meaning something extra or in addition to or including other things.

MIRLITON: A commonly used green Cajun vegetable also referred to as a vegetable pear, chayote or mango squash.

OKRA: A green pod vegetable of African origin used in gumbos and as a side dish.

REDFISH: A reddish colored fish with a dark spot on its tail commonly available in Louisiana's shallow coastal waters; also called channel bass or red drum.

ROUX: A classic Cajun concoction made by blending flour and oil and cooking the two together; used in Cajun gumbos, stews, fricassées, courtbouillons, sauce piquantes and other dishes. (See page 213.)

SALT MEAT: A salty pork meat often used to season Cajun soups and other dishes.

SAUCE PIQUANTE: A hot, spicy Cajun stew made with a roux, tomato sauce and various meats such as hen, geese, duck, rabbits, squirrel or turtle and other meats historically available in Cajun country.

SAUSAGE CASING: A natural casing used in the preparation of boudin, andouille and pork sausages made from the intestines of pork and beef and readily available at most meat markets.

TASSO: A dried, smoked pork used in gumbos and other dishes.

YAMS: Louisiana sweet potatoes; used as a side dish, in pies and otherwise.

Appetizers

APPETIZERS

"APPETIZERS: The Acadians say these little taste treats should be served only to whet one's appetite. Make them tasty and eye-appealing, but serve only a few."

CRAWFISH BALLS

2 pounds of peeled crawfish tails
1 onion, chopped
1 bell pepper, chopped
4 slices of stale bread
2 tablespoons of crawfish fat (if available)
1 egg, beaten
3 tablespoons of chopped parsley
3 tablespoons of chopped green onion tops
Salt, black pepper and cayenne pepper, to taste
1½ cups of bread crumbs

1. Grind crawfish tails, onions, bell pepper and bread slices in food processor or grinder.
2. Add crawfish fat, egg, parsley and green onion tops; mix thoroughly; add salt, black pepper and cayenne pepper and mix.
3. Shape into balls the size of a walnut and roll in bread crumbs.
4. Bake 20 minutes at 350 degrees.

Yield: About 4 dozen

Note: These can be frozen after rolling in bread crumbs and baked without thawing.
If crawfish fat is not available, simply omit it from the recipe.

CRAB MEAT DIVINE

1 large white onion, chopped
6 green onion tops, chopped
3 stalks of celery, finely chopped
½ pound of butter
4 tablespoons of flour
2 cups of evaporated milk
2 egg yolks
2 pounds of fresh white crab meat
Salt and pepper, to taste
White wine

1. Saute onions and celery in butter until soft.
2. Blend in flour; blend in milk.
3. Remove from heat. Add remaining ingredients.
4. Serve in chafing dish with Melba rounds.

SHRIMP BALLS

1 quart of shrimp, peeled and ground
2 medium potatoes, boiled and mashed
1 bell pepper, chopped
1 onion, chopped
1 clove of garlic, minced
1 egg
Salt and pepper, to taste
½ cup of flour
Oil
1 8-ounce can of tomato sauce

1. Mix shrimp, potatoes, half of the bell pepper, half of the onion, garlic and egg; season with salt and pepper.
2. Shape into balls. Roll balls in flour and brown in hot oil; place in skillet with other half of bell pepper and onion; cover with tomato sauce.
3. Simmer for one hour.

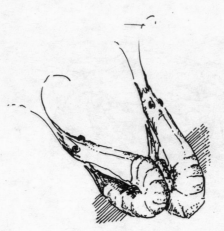

OYSTER CROQUETTES

1 pint of oysters, drained
1 teaspoon of grated onion
1 teaspoon of minced parsley
1 cup of soft bread crumbs
¼ teaspoon of salt
¼ teaspoon of black pepper
Dash of hot pepper sauce
2 eggs, beaten
2 teaspoons of butter or oleo, melted
1 cup of dry bread crumbs

1. Pour boiling water over oysters; drain well; chop fine.
2. Add onion, parsley, soft bread crumbs, salt, pepper and hot sauce; blend this mixture with one beaten egg and the butter.
3. Chill for 20 to 30 minutes.
4. Shape into tiny balls; roll in remaining beaten egg, then in dry bread crumbs.
5. Deep fry in fat at 360 degrees until brown; drain on absorbent paper. Serve hot on toothpicks.

OYSTERS IN PATTY SHELLS

5 dozen oysters (reserve the oyster liquid)
1 onion, chopped fine
3 tablespoons of butter
1 tablespoon of flour
3 tablespoons of chopped parsley
Salt and cayenne pepper, to taste
1 dozen 3-inch patty shells or 36 miniature shells, baked

1. Bring oysters and oyster liquid to a boil; simmer for 10 minutes and drain (reserve liquid).
2. Saute onions in butter until transparent; blend in flour.
3. Add oysters, parsley, salt and cayenne pepper and cook for about 6 minutes; if mixture is too dry, add some of the oyster liquid.
4. Pour into patty shells; bake at 400 degrees for 15 minutes.

Yield: 1 dozen large or 3 dozen bite-size patty shells
Note: If using miniature shells, chop oysters coarsely.

SAUSAGE BALLS

**2 pounds of fresh pork sausage, homemade or
  commercially prepared (See page 96)**
Cayenne pepper, to taste
Biscuit Dough (Recipe follows)
Oil for frying

1. Remove pork from casing; if sausage is not peppered, add cayenne pepper to taste.
2. Shape into small balls the size of walnuts and fry in hot oil at 375 degrees until brown; drain on paper towels.
3. Flour hands and wrap a small piece of biscuit dough around each sausage ball; bake about 18 minutes at 350 degrees.

Yield: About 4 dozen

Biscuit Dough

2 cups of flour
4 teaspoons of baking powder
½ teaspoon of salt
Cayenne pepper, to taste
½ teaspoon of cream of tartar
½ cup of shortening
⅔ cup of milk

1. Sift flour, baking powder, salt, cayenne pepper and cream of tartar together; cut in shortening until mixture resembles coarse cornmeal.
2. Add milk and mix briefly only until flour disappears.

STUFFED BANANA PEPPERS

1 pound of ground meat
1 large onion, finely chopped
1 tablespoon of soy sauce
Salt and pepper, to taste
Banana peppers, split and washed
Eggs, beaten
Flour
Oil for frying

1. Combine meat, onion, soy sauce, salt and pepper; mix very well.
2. Stuff banana peppers with meat mixture. Roll in egg and then into flour; deep fry in oil until golden brown.

BOUDIN BALLS

2 pounds of boudin (See page 104)
2 eggs, beaten
Bread crumbs seasoned with salt and cayenne pepper
Oil for frying

1. Remove boudin from casing; shape mixture into balls about the size of a walnut.
2. Dip in eggs and then into seasoned bread crumbs.
3. Deep fat fry at 375 degrees until golden brown; drain on paper towels.

Yield: About 4 dozen

Breads and Cereals

BREADS AND CEREALS

"The bread may be cornbread, 'lost bread,' corn fritters or a variety of spoon breads. Twenty to thirty years ago couch-couch was commonly served in the Acadian homes with milk or with sausage and a rusty gravy or syrup."

FRENCH BREAD

2¼ cups of warm water (110 degrees)
1 envelope of dry yeast
1 teaspoon of sugar
7 to 8 cups of sifted flour
Salt
1 tablespoon of butter, softened
½ cup of corn meal

1. Combine ¼ cup of the warm water, yeast and sugar and let mixture set for 10 minutes or until mixture doubles in bulk.
2. Add yeast mixture to seven cups of flour, one tablespoon of salt and the remaining two cups of warm water; mix well until the dough can be gathered into a ball.
3. Knead dough, adding more flour if necessary (up to one cup) until dough is no longer sticky.
4. Spread butter on the inside of a large bowl and place dough in bowl, turning dough until surface is coated with butter; cover and let dough stand in a warm place until it doubles in bulk.
5. Punch the dough down and divide into 3 pieces; shape each piece into a loaf about two inches in diameter and 15 inches long and place on a cookie sheet dusted with corn meal. Cut 5 or 6 diagonal slashes across the top of each loaf.
6. Mix ½ teaspoon of salt with ½ cup of water; brush each loaf with the water-salt mixture, cover and let rise until double in bulk.
7. Place large, shallow baking pan half filled with water on the bottom of the oven (or directly on the heating element of an electric oven); bake breads at 400 degrees for 15 minutes.
8. Lower heat to 350 degrees, brush bread with water-salt mixture and continue to bake for 30 minutes (basting again with water-salt mixture) until loaves are golden brown; cool on a wire rack.

Yield: 3 loaves

BRIOCHE

2 envelopes of dry yeast
1 cup plus 2 tablespoons of milk,
   scalded and cooled to 110 degrees
¾ cup of butter
½ cup plus 6 tablespoons of sugar
1 teaspoon of salt
4½ cups of sifted flour
½ teaspoon of lemon extract
4 egg yolks

1. Dissolve yeast in 1 cup of the milk.
2. Cream butter, ½ cup of the sugar and salt together; add to the yeast mixture, mixing well.
3. Add flour and lemon extract, mixing well; add egg yolks, one at a time, beating well after each addition.
4. Continue to beat for 10 minutes; cover and let stand at room temperature for 6 hours. (Mixture will rise and double in bulk.)
5. Stir dough down, cover and refrigerate overnight.
6. Divide dough into small balls about 1½ inches in diameter and put into greased muffin pans or close together in a baking pan; brush top with a mixture of 6 tablespoons of sugar and 2 tablespoons of milk.
7. Bake at 400 degrees for about 20 minutes.

Yield: 2 dozen

CROISSANTS

¾ cup of butter
1¼ cups of flour
3 tablespoons of sugar
1 teaspoon of salt
1 package of yeast
¾ cup plus 1 tablespoon of milk
¼ cup of water
2 eggs
Additional flour and sugar

1. Cut butter into one-fourth cup of flour until smooth; place between two sheets of waxed paper and roll into a 10 × 4 inch rectangle. Chill one hour.
2. In a large bowl, mix one cup of flour, sugar, salt and yeast.
3. Combine three-fourths cup of milk and the water in saucepan; heat until warm.
4. Add to dry ingredients slowly; beat for two minutes.
5. Add one egg and enough flour to make a thick batter; beat two more minutes.
6. Add more flour to make a soft dough; turn out onto a heavily floured board. Roll out to a 12-inch square.
7. Carefully peel waxed paper from chilled butter mixture; place over center one-third of dough; fold one outside one-third of dough over butter slab, then the other one-third.
8. Give dough a quarter turn and roll out to 12-inch square. Repeat the above three more times. Wrap in waxed paper and chill two hours.
9. Divide dough into three pieces and shape one piece at a time. Roll one piece into a 12-inch circle; cut into eight pie-shaped pieces.
10. Beat one egg and one tablespoon of milk together; brush each piece with liquid.
11. Roll, beginning with wide end; brush each piece with liquid and sprinkle with sugar.
12. Let rise in warm place until double in bulk (about one hour).
13. Bake at 375 degrees for about 12 minutes until brown.

Yield: 2 dozen

CORNBREAD

1 cup of yellow corn meal
1 cup of flour
½ teaspoon of salt
¼ cup of sugar (optional)
4 teaspoons of baking powder
1 cup of milk
1 egg
2 tablespoons of butter, melted

1. Combine corn meal, flour, salt, sugar and baking powder; add milk, egg and butter and stir until blended, about one minute.
2. Pour into a greased eight-inch square baking dish and bake at 425 degrees for 20 to 25 minutes or until golden brown; cut into two-inch squares.

Yield: 16 squares of cornbread

SHRIMP CORNBREAD

2 eggs
1 16-ounce can of cream style corn
⅓ cup of oil
½ cup of grated cheddar cheese
1 cup of white corn meal
½ teaspoon of baking soda
1 teaspoon of salt
1 cup of raw shrimp, peeled and deveined
½ cup of chopped onions
Chopped jalapeno peppers, to taste

1. Combine eggs, corn and oil; add cheese and mix.
2. Stir in corn meal, baking soda and salt; add shrimp, onions and jalapeno peppers and mix.
3. Bake at 350 degrees for 45 minutes in a greased 9 × 12 inch pan.

Yield: 24 2-inch squares

CROQUIGNOLES
Doughnuts

¼ cup of butter
1½ cups of sugar
1 teaspoon of vanilla or almond flavoring
3 eggs
1 cup of milk
4 teaspoons of baking powder
Pinch of salt
4 cups of flour
Oil for frying
Granulated or powdered sugar

1. Beat butter until soft; add sugar gradually and beat until mixture is light and fluffy.
2. Add vanilla or almond flavoring and the eggs, one at a time, beating after each addition.
3. Add milk and mix well.
4. Mix baking powder, salt and flour together and add to the egg mixture, mixing well.
5. Place dough on a well-floured board and roll to ½-inch thickness; cut into rounds with a donut cutter.
6. Fry in oil at 375 degrees until lightly brown, turning to brown both sides; drain on paper towels and sprinkle with granulated or powdered sugar.

Yield: About 3 dozen

BEIGNETS

1 cup of water
1 cup of milk
1 egg, beaten
3 cups of flour
2 tablespoons of baking powder
1 teaspoon of salt
2 teaspoons of sugar
Oil for frying
Confectioners sugar

1. Mix water, milk and egg; add flour, baking powder, salt, and 2 teaspoons of sugar and mix until smooth.
2. Drop by spoonfuls into 2 inches of hot oil at 375 degrees; drain on paper towels and sprinkle with confectioners sugar.

Yield: About 2 dozen

PAIN PERDUE
Lost Bread or French Toast

1 5-ounce can of evaporated milk
2 eggs, well beaten
½ cup of sugar
½ teaspoon of vanilla
6 slices of french bread
1 cup of oil or butter
Powdered sugar

1. Mix together evaporated milk, eggs, sugar and vanilla; dip each slice of bread into this mixture, coating well.
2. Drain off excess batter and fry in hot oil at 375 degrees until brown; turn and brown other side.
3. Drain on paper towels and sprinkle with powdered sugar.

Yield: 6 servings

HUSH PUPPIES

1 cup of corn meal
1 cup of flour
1 teaspoon of salt
1 teaspoon of baking powder
1 onion, grated
½ cup of chopped green onion tops
¾ cup of milk
1 egg
Oil for frying

1. Mix all ingredients together until dry ingredients are moistened.
2. Drop by tablespoons into oil at 375 degrees and cook until golden brown.

BISCUITS

2 cups of sifted flour
4 teaspoons of baking powder
¾ teaspoon of salt
¼ cup of shortening or butter
⅔ cup of milk

1. Sift all dry ingredients together; cut in shortening or butter until mixture resembles coarse corn meal.
2. Add milk and mix briefly or until dry ingredients are moistened.
3. Place on a floured board and knead gently about 10 times; roll out to about ½-inch thickness.
4. Place on baking sheet and bake at 450 degrees about 10 minutes or until golden brown.

Yield: 2 dozen biscuits

PUMPKIN BREAD

3 cups of sugar
4 eggs
1 cup of oil
⅔ cup of water
2 cups of cooked pumpkin (or canned)
1½ cups of chopped pecans
3½ cups of flour
1½ teaspoons of salt
2 teaspoons of baking soda
1 teaspoon of nutmeg
1 teaspoon of cinnamon

1. Beat sugar and eggs together; add oil, water, pumpkin and pecans and mix well.
2. Combine remaining ingredients and stir into pumpkin mixture, mixing thoroughly.
3. Bake in two large greased loaf pans, filling pans half full, at 350 degrees for one hour or until golden brown.

COUCHE-COUCHE

2 cups of corn meal
1½ teaspoons of salt
1 teaspoon of baking powder
1½ cups of milk
½ cup of oil

1. Mix corn meal, salt, baking powder and milk; heat oil on medium heat in a heavy pot.
2. Add corn meal mixture to hot oil and let it form a crust, about 5 minutes; stir, lower heat, cover and cook 15 minutes.
3. Serve with milk as a cereal or pour sugar cane syrup over the top; it may also be served with Sucre Brulé.

Yield: 6 servings

SUCRE BRULE

1 cup of sugar
1 cup of water

1. In a heavy pot, cook sugar on medium heat until golden brown and melted, stirring constantly.
2. Add water slowly, continuing to stir and cook until sugar is completely dissolved and mixture is the consistency of a thin syrup.
3. Serve with Couche-Couche or add to boiled milk, adding enough so that milk is beige in color; additional sugar may be added to milk to sweeten it enough.

GRITS

5½ **cups of water**
1 **teaspoon of salt**
3½ **tablespoons of butter**
1 **cup of grits**

1. Bring water to a boil in a heavy saucepan; add salt and butter.
2. Add grits to boiling water, stirring constantly; lower heat, cover pot and cook on low heat for 35 minutes, stirring occasionally.
3. Serve with butter or serve with gravy from Grillades.

GARLIC GRITS

2 **cups of grits**
1 **tablespoon of salt**
2 **quarts of water**
6 **ounces of cheddar cheese, grated**
3 **cloves of garlic, minced**
¼ **pound of butter**
3 **eggs, beaten**
2 **cups of milk**
Grated parmesan cheese

1. Add grits to boiling salted water and cook, covered, until grits are tender but mixture is still pourable, about 20 minutes.
2. Remove from heat and add cheese, garlic and butter; stir until cheese and butter are melted.
3. Cool and add eggs and milk; pour into a large 4-quart greased casserole and bake at 325 degrees for 50 to 60 minutes.
4. Remove from oven, sprinkle with parmesan cheese and return to oven for 10 minutes.

Yield: 8 servings

Note: To prepare ahead of time, mix and pour into casserole and refrigerate. Bake just before serving.

Salads
and
Vegetables

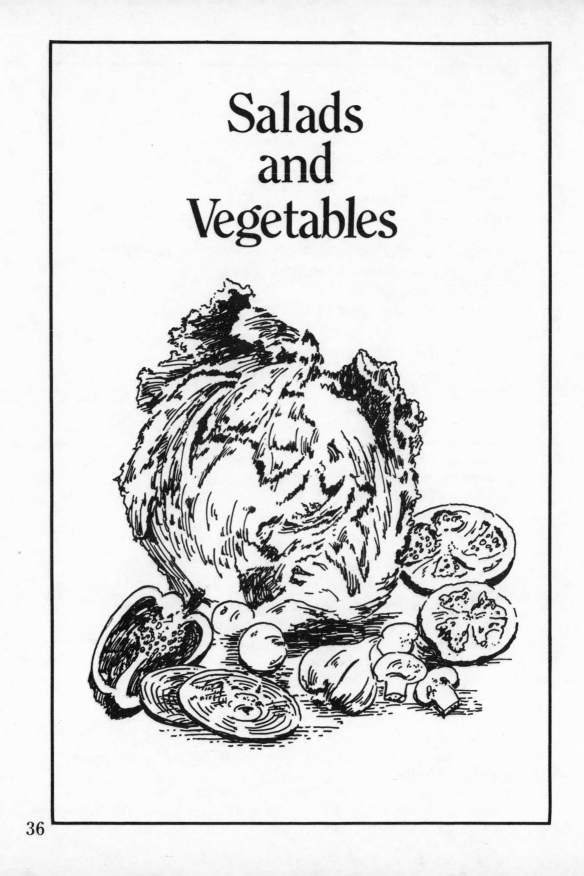

SALADS

VEGETABLES

MARINATED CRAB MEAT SALAD

1 medium onion, chopped fine
1 pound of fresh crab meat
½ cup of oil
6 tablespoons of cider vinegar
½ cup of water
Salt and pepper, to taste
Lettuce leaves

1. Mix all ingredients except lettuce lightly and marinate 12 hours.
2. Serve chilled over lettuce leaves.

Yield: 4 servings

CRAB SALAD

¾ cup of crab meat
2 tablespoons of chopped celery
2 tablespoons of chopped stuffed olives
1 teaspoon of chopped green onions
1 teaspoon of lemon juice
1 tablespoon of mayonnaise
Salt and pepper, to taste
Tomatoes (optional)

1. Mix first seven ingredients together in a bowl.
2. If desired, cut out the insides of the tomatoes, leaving enough pulp to make a firm shell.
3. Stuff with crab mixture.

Yield: 2 servings

SEAFOOD SALAD

3 cups of water
1 pound of shrimp
¼ pound of lump crab meat
¼ cup of chopped celery
½ cup of chopped bell peppers
2½ tablespoons of chopped sweet
   pickles
1 green onion, minced
1½ teaspoons of dried parsley
½ cup of sliced ripe olives
1 cup of Italian salad dressing
2 tablespoons of olive oil
1½ teaspoons of lemon juice
Leaf lettuce
½ medium head of lettuce, coarsely
   shredded
2 medium tomatoes, cut into wedges

1. Bring water to a boil; add shrimp; return to boil. Lower heat and simmer three to five minutes. Drain well; rinse in cold water. Peel and devein shrimp.
2. Combine shrimp and next 10 ingredients; cover in an airtight container; refrigerate overnight.
3. Line platter with leaf lettuce; spoon on shrimp mixture; top with shredded lettuce and garnish with tomato wedges.

Yield: 4 to 6 servings

SHRIMP SALAD

¾ cup of mayonnaise
1 teaspoon of salt
2 teaspoons of dry mustard
6 green onions, minced or diced
2 stalks of celery, minced
1 teaspoon of paprika
2 drops of hot sauce
3 sprigs of parsley, minced
2 pounds of shrimp, boiled and peeled
Lettuce leaves
Hard-boiled eggs, halved

1. Combine first eight ingredients and pour over shrimp; refrigerate for four to six hours.
2. Serve on lettuce leaves and decorate with eggs.

Yield: 6 servings

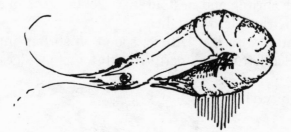

CUCUMBER AND ONION SALAD

1 cup of sour cream
⅓ cup of mayonnaise
¼ cup of cider vinegar
½ teaspoon of dill weed
½ teaspoon of black pepper
Salt, to taste
3 medium or large cucumbers, peeled
and sliced very thin
1 medium white onion, sliced very thin

1. Mix first six ingredients in a small bowl; add cucumbers and onions; mix well.
2. Keep chilled in refrigerator until ready to serve.

Yield: 6 to 8 servings

POTATO SALAD

6 large red potatoes, boiled and peeled
¼ cup of green onion tops
¼ cup of finely chopped celery
¼ cup of finely chopped parsley
6 hard-boiled eggs, peeled
Salt, cayenne pepper and black pepper, to taste
1 cup of mayonnaise
1 tablespoon of prepared mustard

1. Dice potatoes into a large salad bowl; add green onion tops, celery and parsley.
2. Separate cooked egg whites from yolks; chop white and add to potatoes.
3. Mash yolks and mix with mayonnaise and mustard; add this mixture to potatoes and mix well. (Add more mayonnaise if salad appears too dry.)
4. Season with salt and pepper to taste.

Yield: 6 to 8 servings

COLESLAW

1 head of cabbage, shredded
4 carrots, peeled and grated
3 cups of mayonnaise
2 cups of red wine vinegar
Salt and black pepper, to taste

1. Combine cabbage and carrots in a large bowl; mix mayonnaise and vinegar together with a wire whip until well blended.
2. Add mayonnaise mixture to cabbage mixture and mix well.
3. Season to taste with salt and black pepper.

Yield: 12 servings

ACORN SQUASH

1 acorn squash, cut in half and cleaned
½ cup of butter
2 tablespoons of brown sugar
Cinnamon

1. Steam squash, cut side down, in a large covered pot with a small amount of water for 20 minutes.
2. Remove from pan and place in a casserole dish.
3. Top with slices of butter and brown sugar; sprinkle with cinnamon and bake 15 minutes at 350 degrees.

Yield: 2 servings

YELLOW SQUASH WITH HAM

12 yellow squash, sliced
1 large onion, chopped
1 stalk of celery, chopped
1 bell pepper, chopped
½ cup of butter
2 eggs, beaten
1 teaspoon of salt
1 teaspoon of minced garlic
2 teaspoons of monosodium glutamate
1 pound of diced smoked ham
Bread crumbs

1. Boil squash in lightly salted water to cover until tender; drain and mash.
2. Saute onion, celery and bell pepper in butter until onions are transparent; add sauteed vegetables to squash.
3. Add eggs, salt, garlic, monosodium glutamate and ham; place in buttered casserole and top with bread crumbs and dot with butter.
4. Bake at 350 degrees for 20 minutes.

Yield: 8 servings

BAKED CUSHAW (SQUASH)

1 medium cushaw (squash)
3 eggs
1 cup of sugar
2 tablespoons of flour
2 teaspoons of nutmeg
2 teaspoons of vanilla
½ teaspoon of salt
¾ stick of butter

1. Peel cushaw, remove all seeds and stringy parts and cut it up; boil in small amount of water until tender, about 30 to 45 minutes. Drain water.
2. Add all remaining ingredients except butter.
3. Put butter in casserole and melt; pour cushaw mixture into butter.
4. Bake uncovered at 325 degrees until done, about 30 minutes.

Yield: 4 to 6 servings

RED KIDNEY BEANS

1 pound of red kidney beans
1 pound of salt meat
1 large onion, chopped
1 quart of water
1 clove of garlic, minced
Salt and cayenne pepper, to taste

1. Soak beans in water to cover overnight; drain.
2. Boil salt meat in water to cover and drain; repeat this procedure two more times. This removes the excess salt from the meat.
3. Combine beans, salt meat, onion, water, garlic, salt and cayenne pepper; bring to a boil, lower heat and simmer for 1½ to 2 hours or until beans are tender.

Yield: 6 servings

BUTTER BEANS

2 onions, chopped
1 clove of garlic, chopped
½ cup of bacon drippings
Salt and cayenne pepper, to taste
1 ham bone or ½ pound of ham
½ cup of chopped green onions
½ cup of chopped parsley
2½ pounds of fresh or dried butter beans
2½ quarts of water

1. Saute onions and garlic in bacon drippings until onions are transparent; add remaining ingredients.
2. Bring to a boil, lower heat and simmer until beans are tender and creamy, about 45 minutes for fresh beans and 1½ hours for dried. (It may be necessary to add more water if beans start to stick or become dry.)

Yield: 8 servings

LIMA BEANS AND SHRIMP

¼ cup of oil
¼ cup of flour
2 onions, chopped
2 cans of lima beans or 2 packages of frozen lima beans
1 pound of shrimp, peeled and deveined
Water

1. Make a roux with oil and flour; saute onions until transparent.
2. Add lima beans, shrimp and water as necessary and cook 30 to 40 minutes.

Yield: 6 to 8 servings

CAULIFLOWER AU GRATIN

1 whole cauliflower
2 teaspoons of prepared mustard
½ teaspoon of salt
¾ cup of mayonnaise
¾ cup of grated sharp cheddar cheese
Paprika

1. Boil cauliflower in water to cover until tender; break into flowerettes and place in a casserole dish.
2. Mix mustard, salt and mayonnaise; spread evenly over cauliflower.
3. Top with cheese and bake at 325 degrees until cheese is melted; sprinkle with paprika.

Yield: 8 servings

CORN PUDDING

3 tablespoons of butter
¼ cup of chopped onion
½ bell pepper, chopped
2 cups of fresh corn (or 2 cups
  of drained canned corn)
2 tablespoons of sugar
1 teaspoon of salt
Black pepper, to taste
½ cup of grated cheddar cheese
3 eggs, beaten

1. Melt butter in skillet; saute onion and bell pepper in butter until onions are transparent.
2. Add corn, sugar, salt and black pepper and cook 15 to 20 minutes on medium-low heat; cool slightly and add cheese and eggs.
3. Place in a casserole dish and bake at 350 degrees for 35 minutes.

Yield: 6 servings

SCALLOPED CORN

1 17-ounce can of cream-style corn
2 tablespoons of chopped pimento
1 teaspoon of grated onion
1 beaten egg
½ teaspoon of salt
⅛ teaspoon of pepper
¾ cup of cracker crumbs
2 tablespoons of butter

1. Combine all ingredients except butter and one-fourth cup of cracker crumbs; spread evenly in an eight-inch square pan.
2. Melt butter, mix with remaining cracker crumbs, toss lightly and sprinkle over mix.
3. Bake uncovered at 350 degrees for 20 minutes or until set in center.

Yield: 4 servings

MAQUE CHOUX

1 dozen ears of fresh corn on the cob
2 tablespoons of oil or butter
1 onion, chopped
½ bell pepper, chopped
Salt and cayenne pepper, to taste

1. Cut corn off the cob by slicing across the tops of the kernels thinly and then cutting across a second time to remove the "milk" from the corn.
2. Heat oil in a heavy pot and add corn and remaining ingredients; cook on medium-low heat for 20 minutes, stirring constantly to keep corn from sticking.
3. Lower heat, cover pot and continue to cook for a few more minutes, about 5 minutes.

Yield: 8 servings

MAQUE CHOUX WITH TOMATOES

12 ears of fresh corn on the cob
½ pound of butter
1 large onion, chopped
½ bell pepper, chopped
2 large tomatoes, peeled and chopped
½ cup of water
Salt and cayenne pepper, to taste

1. Cut corn from cob by scraping knife across the top of the kernels; scrape across the kernels a second time to remove the "milk" from the corn and reserve the corn mixture.
2. Melt butter in a heavy pot; saute onions and bell pepper until onions are transparent.
3. Add corn, tomatoes and water; cover and simmer about 12 minutes.
4. Add salt and cayenne pepper and simmer another 15 minutes or until corn is tender.

Yield: 8 servings

SNAP BEANS WITH POTATOES

6 slices of bacon
3 tablespoons of butter
1 large onion, chopped
1 pound of fresh snap beans or green beans
2 cups of water
½ pound of chopped smoked ham
Salt and cayenne pepper, to taste
12 new potatoes, peeled

1. Fry bacon until crisp; remove bacon and add butter to bacon drippings.
2. Add onions and saute until onions are transparent; add beans, water, ham, salt and cayenne pepper and bring to a boil.
3. Lower heat and simmer beans, covered, for 50 minutes or until beans are almost tender; add potatoes and continue to cook about 20 to 25 minutes or until potatoes are fork tender.

Yield: 6 servings

SNAP BEANS WITH ROUX

1 tablespoon of flour
1 tablespoon of oil
1 small onion, chopped
1 16-ounce can of snap beans or green beans
Salt and cayenne pepper, to taste

1. Make a dark brown roux with flour and oil; add onions and cook until onions are transparent.
2. Add juice from canned beans and stir until roux is dissolved; add beans, salt and cayenne pepper and cook on low heat until gravy in beans is the consistency of thick cream, about 30 minutes.

Yield: 3 to 4 servings

FRIED OKRA

2 pounds of okra, cut into ¾-inch pieces
Salt and cayenne pepper
1 cup of flour
1 cup of white corn meal
2 eggs, beaten
Oil for frying

1. Season okra with salt and cayenne pepper; combine flour and corn meal and season with more salt and cayenne pepper.
2. Dip okra into egg and then into flour-corn meal mixture.
3. Fry in deep oil at 375 degrees until golden brown, about 5 minutes or less; drain on paper towels.
4. Serve as a side dish with any meat or seafood.

Yield: 6 to 8 servings

SMOTHERED OKRA

1 large onion, chopped
1 tomato, peeled and chopped
½ cup of oil
2 pounds of fresh okra, sliced ½-inch thick
Salt, black pepper and cayenne pepper, to taste

1. Saute onion and tomato together in oil about two minutes.
2. Add okra, stir well and cook on medium heat in a partially covered pot about 45 minutes or until okra is no longer ropey.
3. Season with salt, black pepper and cayenne pepper.

Yield: 6 to 8 servings

EGGPLANT FRITTERS

1 pound of eggplant, peeled and cubed
1 teaspoon of baking powder
⅓ cup of flour
1 teaspoon of sugar
⅛ teaspoon of nutmeg
1 teaspoon of salt
Oil for frying

1. Cook eggplant in a large, heavy skillet, adding just enough water to keep eggplant from sticking to the bottom of the pot; when eggplant is tender, mash with a fork.
2. Add remaining ingredients except oil and beat with a fork until well-mixed.
3. Drop mixture by spoonfuls into hot, deep oil at 350 degrees and cook until golden brown; drain on paper towels.

Yield: 6 servings

SMOTHERED EGGPLANT

½ cup of butter
2 large onions, chopped
1 bell pepper, chopped
3 fresh tomatoes, sliced
1 large eggplant, peeled and sliced ¾ inch thick
** and soaked in cold, salted water**
2 cloves of garlic, mashed
1 teaspoon of salt
½ teaspoon of hot sauce

1. Melt butter over low heat; saute onions and bell pepper until onions are transparent.
2. Add tomatoes; cook very slowly for about 20 minutes; stir occasionally.
3. Add eggplant, garlic, salt and hot sauce; cover and steam for about 30 minutes.

Yield: 6 servings

FRIED SWEET POTATOES

1 29-ounce can of sweet potatoes
½ cup of sugar
Oil for frying

1. Drain sweet potatoes well; slice into ½-inch pieces and sprinkle both sides with a small amount of the sugar.
2. Fry in hot oil at 350 degrees until lightly brown; drain on paper towels and sprinkle with more sugar.
3. Serve with pork or any meat dish.

Yield: 4 to 6 servings

SWEET POTATO PIE

6 medium sweet potatoes
1 cup of sugar
2 eggs, beaten
¼ teaspoon of grated nutmeg

1. Boil sweet potatoes in water to cover until tender, about 30 minutes; peel and mash.
2. Add sugar, eggs and nutmeg; mix well.
3. Pour into a buttered glass pie plate; bake at 375 degrees for 50 to 60 minutes.
4. Serve cold, cut into pie-shaped pieces.

Yield: 8 servings

Note: Serve as a side dish with any meat or poultry.

CAJUN SWEET POTATOES

6 to 8 sweet potatoes
2 cups of sugar
¼ cup of water
¼ cup of butter
1 teaspoon of cinnamon

1. Bake sweet potatoes at 350 degrees for about one hour; cool, peel and slice and place in a baking dish.
2. Mix sugar, water, butter and cinnamon in a saucepan; bring to a boil and boil for 15 minutes.
3. Pour syrup over sweet potatoes and bake 45 minutes at 350 degrees.

Yield: 8 servings

CANDIED SWEET POTATOES

1 29-ounce can of sweet potatoes
2 cups of sugar
¼ cup of butter

1. Drain juice from sweet potatoes; combine juice with sugar and cook on medium heat for 10 minutes.
2. Place sweet potatoes in a casserole dish, pour syrup over the top and place butter pats over the potatoes.
3. Bake at 350 degrees about 30 minutes or until syrup is thick, basting sweet potatoes often.

Yield: 4 servings

PRALINE-TOPPED SWEET POTATOES

8 sweet potatoes
2 cups of chopped pecans
1 cup of brown sugar
¾ cup of oleo
Pinch of salt
1 teaspoon of vanilla

1. Bake sweet potatoes at 350 degrees for about one hour; peel, slice and place in a buttered 9 × 13 inch baking dish.
2. Mix together pecans, brown sugar, oleo, salt and vanilla in a saucepan; bring to a boil and cook for about two to three minutes.
3. Pour over potatoes and bake at 350 degrees for 10 minutes.

Yield: 8 servings

CAJUN POTATO CAKES

5 pounds of red potatoes, peeled and chopped
Salt, black pepper and cayenne pepper, to taste
1 onion, grated
2 eggs
Flour
Oil for frying

1. Boil potatoes in salted water to cover about 20 minutes.
2. Drain potatoes and mash well, adding salt, black pepper, cayenne pepper, onion and eggs; mix well.
3. Shape into cakes about two inches in diameter and one-half inch thick; roll in flour.
4. Place in refrigerator overnight.
5. Re-dust with flour; fry in ½-inch of oil in a teflon-coated skillet turning once until brown on each side.

Yield: 24 cakes

FRIED ONION RINGS

1 egg, beaten
1⅔ cups of milk
1 cup of flour
¾ teaspoon of baking powder
½ teaspoon of salt
Cayenne pepper, to taste
2 large onions, sliced in ¼-inch slices and separated into rings
Oil for frying

1. Combine egg, ⅔ cup of the milk, flour, baking powder, salt and cayenne pepper and mix well; refrigerate for 30 minutes.
2. Soak onion rings in 1 cup of the milk for 30 minutes; drain.
3. Dip onion rings into batter and fry at 375 degrees until golden brown; drain on paper towels.

Yield: 4 servings

CRAB-STUFFED POTATOES

4 large white potatoes
¾ cup of butter or oleo
¾ cup of whipping or light cream
Cayenne pepper, to taste
½ teaspoon of garlic powder
2 tablespoons of grated onions
¼ cup of chopped parsley
¼ cup of chopped green onions
½ teaspoon of salt
1 to 1½ cups of grated sharp yellow cheese
1 pound of white crab meat
Paprika

1. Scrub potatoes; dry thoroughly. Bake at 325 degrees until you can easily pierce with fork (about one and a half hours).
2. Cut lengthwise; scoop out potatoes, leaving enough potato to hold shell firmly together.
3. Whip potato with butter, cream, pepper, garlic powder, onion, parsley, green onion, salt and cheese; mix crab meat into this lightly.
4. Refill the potato shells with mixture; sprinkle generously with paprika.
5. Reheat at 400 degrees for 20 to 25 minutes.

Yield: 8 servings

Note: These can be served on a bed of lettuce with a few sprigs of parsley for decoration.

MUSTARD GREENS

Bacon or ham, to taste
1 medium onion, chopped
1 bunch of mustard greens, cleaned and chopped
1 quart of water
1 tablespoon of roux
Pinch of sugar
Salt and pepper, to taste

1. Fry bacon; remove bacon and saute onions in bacon drippings until transparent.
2. Add bacon, onions and drippings to all other ingredients in a large pot.
3. Cook until greens are tender, about 15 to 20 minutes.

Yield: 4 to 6 servings

SMOTHERED CABBAGE

1 large cabbage, cut into large pieces with core removed
1 tablespoon of oil
1 large onion, chopped
Pinch of baking soda
Salt, black pepper and cayenne pepper, to taste

1. In a heavy saucepan, place all ingredients and add water to come half-way up cabbage.
2. Boil until all of the water evaporates and continue cooking until cabbage starts to brown. Cabbage will have the appearance of mashed vegetables.

Yield: 6 servings

Gumbos
Soups
Bisques

GUMBOS, SOUPS AND BISQUES

"GUMBO: This dish would be termed a hearty, soupy stew. Conserving the wealth of one's findings has always been a trait of the Acadians. Upon their arrival in south Louisiana, they found an abundance and a variety of seafood. Being conservative and possessing a great deal of ingenuity, they concocted the delectable dish, gumbo. It was soon discovered that a gumbo could be prepared by the use of fowl, wild game, sausage, andouille, chitterlings and "tasso" (a slim piece of smoked meat)."

CRAWFISH BISQUE

¾ **cup of flour**
¾ **cup of oil**
5 medium onions, chopped
6 cloves of garlic, minced
2 stalks of celery, chopped
1 16-ounce can of whole tomatoes, chopped
¼ **cup of tomato sauce**
1 cup of crawfish fat (if available)
3 pounds of peeled crawfish tails, ground
1½ cups of water
Bread crumbs
Salt, black pepper, and cayenne pepper, to taste
155 cleaned crawfish heads
Bisque (Recipe follows)

1. Make a light brown roux with flour and oil; add onions, garlic, celery, tomatoes and tomato sauce and cook, stirring constantly, about 15 minutes.
2. Add crawfish fat and cook an additional 5 minutes; add ground crawfish tails and water and simmer 20 minutes.
3. Remove from heat and cool about 20 minutes; add salt, black pepper, cayenne pepper and enough bread crumbs to make mixture stiff.
4. Stuff crawfish heads and sprinkle tops with bread crumbs; bake at 350 degrees for 30 minutes.
5. To serve, place stuffed heads in a large soup bowl and pour Bisque gravy over the top; serve with cooked rice.

Note: If crawfish fat is not available, add ½ cup of butter and proceed as instructed.

Bisque

1½ cups of flour
1½ cups of oil
4 onions, chopped
3 stalks of celery, chopped
4 cloves of garlic, minced
1 bell pepper, chopped
1 16-ounce can of whole tomatoes, chopped
6 quarts of water
Salt and cayenne pepper to taste
1½ cups of crawfish fat (if available)
2 pounds of peeled crawfish tails

1. Make a roux with flour and oil; add onions, celery, garlic, bell pepper and tomatoes and cook for about seven minutes over medium heat, stirring constantly.
2. Add water, salt and cayenne pepper; bring to a boil, lower heat and simmer for about 45 minutes.
3. Add crawfish fat and simmer 20 minutes; add crawfish tails and continue cooking for about 15 minutes.

Yield: 12 servings

Note: If crawfish fat is not available, add ¾ cup of butter and proceed as instructed.

CHICKEN GUMBO FILE

¾ cup of oil
½ cup of flour
1 onion, chopped
¼ cup of chopped celery
1 chicken, cut into serving pieces
6 cups of water
2 tablespoons of salt
2 tablespoons of black pepper
½ cup of chopped parsley
½ cup of chopped green onions
2 dozen fresh oysters
½ teaspoon of gumbo filé

1. In a large, heavy pot, make a dark brown roux with ½ cup of oil and flour; add onions and celery and cook until onions are transparent.
2. In a large skillet, brown chicken in the remaining ¼ cup of oil; when brown add chicken to roux and cooked vegetables.
3. Add hot water slowly, stirring well to dissolve roux; season with salt and pepper and cook on low heat until chicken is tender, about 45 minutes.
4. Add parsley, green onions and oysters; cook only until oysters start to curl at the edges, approximately 5 minutes.
5. Remove from heat; add filé and serve over cooked rice in soup bowls.

Yield: 4 to 6 servings

CHICKEN-OKRA GUMBO

1 chicken, cut into serving pieces
Salt, black pepper and cayenne pepper, to taste
¼ cup of oil
2½ pounds of fresh okra, cut into ½-inch pieces
  (or 2 16-ounce cans of okra)
2 onions, chopped
1 clove of garlic, minced
¼ cup of flour
1 quart of water

1. Season chicken with salt, black pepper and cayenne pepper; brown in oil in a large, heavy pot. Remove chicken as it browns.
2. Add okra, onions and garlic to the pot and sprinkle flour over the top; stir constantly and cook over low heat until oil starts to rise to the top, about 20 minutes.
3. Add chicken and water and simmer until chicken is tender and the gumbo is the consistency of a cream soup, about one hour.
4. Serve over cooked rice in soup bowls.

Yield: 6 servings

CHICKEN-OYSTER GUMBO

1 chicken, cut into serving pieces
Salt, black pepper and cayenne pepper, to taste
½ cup of oil
½ cup of flour
1 large onion, chopped
2 stalks of celery, chopped
½ bell pepper, chopped
2 quarts of hot water
1 dozen oysters and oyster juice
¼ cup of chopped parsley
¼ cup of chopped green onion tops
Gumbo filé, to taste

1. Season chicken with salt, black pepper and cayenne pepper; brown in oil in a large, heavy pot and remove when each piece browns.
2. Add flour to oil and make a dark brown roux; add onion, celery and bell pepper and cook until onions are transparent.
3. Return chicken to roux and add hot water, stirring until roux is dissolved; cook on low heat for one hour or until chicken is tender.
4. Season gumbo again, if necessary, with salt, black pepper and cayenne pepper; add oysters and oyster juice and continue to cook for about 15 minutes.
5. Add parsley and green onion tops; serve over cooked rice in soup bowls with gumbo filé sprinkled on top, if desired.

Yield: 6 to 8 servings

CHICKEN SAUCE PIQUANTE

1 large hen, cut into serving pieces
½ cup of oil
2 large onions, chopped
2 tablespoons of minced garlic
1 6-ounce can of tomato paste
2 tablespoons of prepared roux
Water
Salt, black pepper and cayenne pepper, to taste
½ cup of white wine
½ cup of chopped parsley
½ cup of chopped green onion tops

1. In a large, heavy pot, brown hen in oil over medium heat; continue to cook, adding a litte water from time to time to prevent sticking.
2. When brown, add onions and garlic and cook until transparent.
3. Add tomato paste, roux, water and seasonings; simmer over a low heat until hen is tender.
4. Fifteen minutes before serving, add wine, parsley and green onion tops; serve over cooked rice in soup bowls.

Yield: 6 to 8 servings

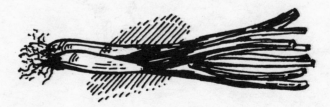

HEN AND SAUSAGE GUMBO

1 large hen, cut into 8 pieces
1 cup of oil
4 quarts of water
1 cup of chopped onions
½ cup of chopped parsley
2 pounds of smoked sausage
1 teaspoon of filé

1. In heavy iron pot fry hen to a deep brown in hot oil; remove oil.
2. Add three quarts of water and chopped vegetables; boil until meat is tender, about 1½ hours.
3. Boil sausage in one quart of water for 20 minutes.
4. Add sausage and water to iron pot; boil about 30 minutes more.
5. Remove from heat. Add filé.
6. Serve over hot rice in soup bowls.

Yield: 8 servings

CRAB SOUP

1½ cups of butter
4 small onions, grated
1 bay leaf
¼ cup of chopped celery leaves
Pinch of thyme
2 cloves of garlic, minced
1 8-ounce can of tomato sauce
½ cup of flour
2 quarts of water
2 pounds of fresh crab meat
Salt and cayenne pepper, to taste
½ cup of chopped parsley
Lemon slices (garnish)

1. Melt butter in a large saucepan; add onions and cook until onions are transparent.
2. Add bay leaf, celery leaves, thyme and garlic and mix well; add tomato sauce and mix again.
3. Stir in flour and mix until well blended; slowly add water, stirring, until mixture is well blended; add crab meat, salt and pepper, bring to a boil and simmer about 10 to 15 minutes. (Be careful not to break up crab meat.)
4. Serve in soup bowls, sprinkled with parsley and topped with lemon slices.

Yield: 8 servings

SHRIMP AND CRAB GUMBO

¾ cup of oil
¾ cup of flour
1 small bell pepper, chopped
1 large onion, chopped
1 stalk of celery, chopped
4 cups of water
Salt, black pepper and cayenne pepper, to taste
1 pound of peeled and deveined shrimp
1 pound of crab meat
½ cup of chopped parsley
½ cup of chopped green onion tops

1. Make a dark brown roux with oil and flour; add bell pepper, onion and celery and cook until onions are transparent.
2. Gradually add the water and continue cooking for at least one hour.
3. Adjust seasoning to taste; add shrimp, crab, parsley and green onion tops and simmer for 10 minutes.
4. Serve over cooked rice in soup bowls.

Yield: 6 to 8 servings

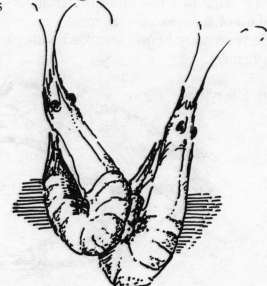

BAYOU SAUCE PIQUANTE

½ cup of cooking oil
2 tablespoons of flour
½ cup of onion, chopped
½ cup of celery, chopped
½ cup of parsley, chopped
2 pounds of shrimp, peeled and deveined
1 16-ounce can of tomato sauce
1 8-ounce can of tomato juice
1 pound of crab meat
1 pound of catfish filets

1. Make a roux with oil and flour; add onion, celery and parsley and cook until wilted.
2. Add tomato sauce and tomato juice; cook about one hour.
3. Add crab meat and catfish and cook another hour, stirring frequently; add shrimp and cook 10 minutes longer.
4. Serve over cooked rice in soup bowls.

Yield: 8 servings

SHRIMP AND OKRA GUMBO

¼ cup of oil
4 pounds of fresh okra, cut in ½-inch pieces
   (or 5 16-ounce cans)
1 tomato, peeled and chopped
2 onions, chopped
2 quarts of water
Salt, black pepper, and cayenne pepper, to taste
3 pounds of peeled and deveined shrimp

1. In oil, cook okra, tomato and onions until okra is no longer ropey, about 45-60 minutes.
2. Add water, salt, black pepper and cayenne pepper and simmer for 30 minutes.
3. Add shrimp and continue to cook another 10 minutes; serve in soup bowls over cooked rice.

Yield: 6 servings

SHRIMP GUMBO

1 cup of flour
½ cup of oil
1 large onion, chopped
2 cups of cubed and washed salt meat
1 cup plus 1 quart of water
2 cups of smoked sausage
3 cups of peeled raw shrimp
Parsley and onion tops, chopped
   (optional)
Salt, to taste
Hot sauce (optional)
¼ teaspoon of gumbo filé

1. Make a brown roux of the flour and oil.
2. Add onions and salt meat; cook until dark brown.
3. Add about one cup of water and the smoked sausage; cook about one-half hour.
4. Add shrimp; cook another half hour.
5. Add parsley, onion tops, salt and hot sauce, if desired.
6. Add one quart of water and bring to a boil; boil slowly for about one-half hour.
7. When you turn off the heat, add filé.
8. Serve over cooked rice in soup bowls.

Yield: 4 to 6 servings

SHRIMP SAUCE PIQUANTE

4 onions, finely chopped
3 bell peppers, finely chopped
1½ cups of chopped green onion tops
1½ cups of chopped parsley
½ cup of oil
1 6-ounce can of tomato paste
1 10-ounce can of tomatoes with chilies
Pinch of sugar
1 cup of water
2 pounds of peeled and deveined shrimp
Salt, black pepper and cayenne pepper, to taste

1. Saute onions, bell pepper, one-half of the green onion tops and one-half of the parsley in oil until onions are transparent; add tomato paste, tomatoes with chilies, sugar and water and cook on low heat for 3 to 4 hours.
2. Add shrimp, remaining green onion tops, parsley, salt, and cayenne pepper; continue to cook for about 20 minutes.
3. Serve over cooked rice in soup bowls.

Yield: 4 to 6 servings

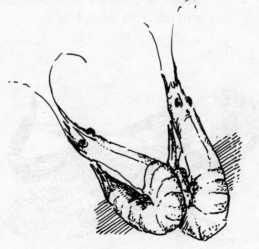

CORN SOUP WITH SHRIMP

5 tablespoons of oil
5 tablespoons of flour
2 onions, chopped
2 bell peppers, chopped
3 cloves of garlic, minced
4 stalks of celery, chopped
1 10-ounce can of tomatoes with chilies
1 16-ounce can of stewed tomatoes
3 16-ounce cans of whole kernel corn
1 16-ounce can of cream style corn
1 gallon of water
Salt, black pepper and cayenne pepper, to taste
2 pounds of shrimp, peeled and deveined
½ cup of chopped green onion tops

1. Make a light brown roux with oil and flour; add onion, bell pepper, garlic, celery, tomatoes with chilies and stewed tomatoes; simmer about 10 minutes.
2. Add whole kernel corn and cream style corn, mixing well; add water, salt, black pepper and cayenne pepper and simmer for one hour.
3. Add shrimp and continue to cook for an additional 10 minutes; add green onion tops and serve in soup bowls.

Yield: 8 to 10 servings

SEAFOOD GUMBO

1 cup of butter
2 cups of flour
6 quarts of water
1 10-ounce can of tomatoes with chilies
2 stalks of celery, chopped
3 onions, chopped
1 bell pepper, chopped
1 clove of garlic, minced
4 pounds of peeled and deveined shrimp
1 pound of crab meat
1 pint of oysters and oyster liquid
Salt, black pepper and cayenne pepper, to taste

1. Make a dark brown roux with butter and flour; add water, bring to a boil and cook until roux is dissolved.
2. Reduce heat to medium and add tomatoes with chilies, celery, onions, bell pepper and garlic; chop enough shrimp to make one cup and add to gumbo.
3. Simmer on low heat for 3 hours.
4. Add remaining shrimp and simmer for 10 minutes; add crab meat, oysters (and oyster liquid), salt, black pepper and cayenne pepper and simmer for another 10 minutes.
5. Serve over cooked rice in soup bowls.

Yield: 10 to 12 servings

OYSTER SOUP

1 onion, chopped
2 stalks of celery, chopped
½ bell pepper, chopped
¼ cup of butter
3 dozen oysters with oyster juice
¼ cup of chopped parsley
¼ cup of chopped green onion tops
¼ cup of chopped celery leaves
1 quart of milk, boiled
Salt, cayenne pepper and hot pepper sauce, to taste

1. Saute onions, celery and bell pepper in butter until onions are transparent; add oysters with oyster juice and simmer for 10 minutes.
2. Add parsley, green onion tops and celery leaves; remove from heat and add remaining ingredients.

Yield: 6 servings

GUMBO Z'HERBES
Mustard Green Gumbo

1½ pounds of salt meat
3 bunches of fresh mustard greens (or spinach, turnip tops
   or beet tops)
2 onions, chopped
1 large white potato, peeled and grated
3 tablespoons of flour
3 tablespoons of oil
2 quarts of water
Cayenne pepper, to taste

1. Boil salt meat in water to cover for about 30 minutes; drain.
2. Boil fresh mustard greens (or spinach, turnip tops or beet tops) in water to cover for about 10 minutes. (Cook frozen mustard greens according to package directions.)
3. Grind mustard greens, salt meat, onions and potatoes together in the food processor or grinder.
4. Make a light brown roux with flour and oil; add roux to mustard green mixture in a large heavy pot.
5. Add water and simmer about 1½ hours; serve in a soup bowl over cooked rice.

Yield: 6 servings

BOUILLABAISSE

1 cup of oil
6 pounds of cleaned fish (redfish or red snapper)
Salt and cayenne pepper, to taste
3 onions, chopped
1 16-ounce can of whole tomatoes, chopped
2 cloves of garlic, minced
1 small bell pepper, chopped

1. Pour oil into a heavy, large pot, coating sides well; season fish with salt and cayenne pepper.
2. In the pot, layer fish, onions, tomatoes, garlic and bell pepper; continue to layer these ingredients until all the fish has been used, finishing with a layer of onions and tomatoes.
3. Cover pot and put on a very low heat to cook for 2 hours. Do not stir.
4. Serve over cooked rice in soup bowls.

Yield: 12 servings

CATFISH COURTBOUILLON

¾ cup of flour
¾ cup of oil
4 onions, chopped
3 stalks of celery, chopped
4 cloves of garlic, minced
1 large bell pepper, chopped
1 16-ounce can of whole tomatoes, chopped
2 cups of water
8 to 10 catfish filets, 1¾ inches thick
Salt, black pepper and cayenne pepper, to taste

1. Make a light brown roux with flour and oil; add onions, celery, garlic, bell pepper, and tomatoes; add water and simmer for about 1½ hours.
2. Season fish with salt, black pepper and cayenne pepper and add to courtbouillon; cook gently for about 10 minutes, covered. Do not stir after the fish has been added; gently shake the pot during the 10 minutes of cooking.
3. Serve over cooked rice in soup bowls.

Yield: 8 to 10 servings

FISH COURTBOUILLON

1 cup of butter
1 cup of flour
3 large onions, chopped
1 cup of chopped celery
3 cloves of garlic, minced
1 16-ounce can of tomatoes
2 6-ounce cans of tomato paste
2½ quarts of water
4 pounds of fish (catfish, redfish or red snapper)
Salt, black pepper and cayenne pepper, to taste
Red wine
2 tablespoons of chopped parsley
2 tablespoons of chopped green onion tops

1. Make a dark brown roux of butter and flour; add onions, celery and garlic and cook until onions are transparent.
2. Add tomatoes and tomato paste and cook slowly, stirring, for 5 minutes; add water and simmer for one hour.
3. Season fish with salt, black pepper and cayenne pepper and dip in red wine; add to tomato sauce and cook on low heat about 15 minutes, without stirring.
4. Add parsley and green onion tops about 5 minutes before serving; serve over cooked rice in soup bowls.

Yield: 6 servings

TURTLE SOUP

1 pound of turtle meat, cut into bite-size pieces
3 tablespoons of butter
3 tablespoons of flour
1 large onion, chopped
1 clove of garlic, minced
½ cup of canned tomatoes, chopped
3 quarts of boiling water
1 teaspoon of thyme
2 whole cloves
Pinch of allspice
Pinch of nutmeg
Salt and black pepper, to taste
2 tablespoons of chopped parsley
2 hard-boiled eggs, chopped
1 lemon, thinly sliced
Sherry (optional)

1. Saute turtle in butter until brown and remove from pan; add flour and stir until a dark brown roux is made.
2. Add onions and garlic and cook until onions are transparent; add tomatoes and cook for 15 minutes, stirring often.
3. Add turtle, boiling water, thyme, cloves, allspice, nutmeg, salt, black pepper and parsley; simmer on low heat for two hours.
4. Serve in soup bowls and garnish with chopped eggs, lemon slices and a splash of sherry, if desired.

Yield: 6 servings

WHITE NAVY BEAN SOUP

1 pound of dried white navy beans
2 one-inch slices of smoked ham
1 large onion, chopped
2 cloves of garlic, minced
2 stalks of celery, cut into one-inch pieces
Salt, black pepper and cayenne pepper, to taste
½ cup of chopped green onion tops (for garnish)

1. Wash beans and cover with water two inches over top; soak overnight.
2. Add ham, onion, garlic and celery; bring to a boil, lower heat and simmer until beans are tender, about one hour. (Additional water may be added if mixture is too thick.)
3. Puree mixture in food processor or blender; return to pot and season to taste with salt, black pepper and cayenne pepper.
4. Add green onion tops and serve in soup bowls.

Yield: 6 servings

Beef
Pork
Lamb

BEEF

PORK

LAMB

STUFFED EGGPLANT

4 eggplants
1 pound of ground meat
1 tablespoon of oil
2 large onions, chopped
½ bell pepper, chopped
2 tablespoons of chopped green onions
1 tablespoon of parsley
Bread crumbs
Salt and pepper, to taste
Butter

1. Cut eggplants in half, scoop out the pulp and save the shells.
2. Boil the pulp of the eggplant until tender, about 30 minutes; drain.
3. Brown the ground meat in oil; add onions, bell pepper, green onions, parsley and eggplant pulp; cook about 20 minutes.
4. Add enough bread crumbs for mixture to be firm; salt and pepper to taste.
5. Stuff eggplant shells with mixture, sprinkle with bread crumbs and dot with butter.
6. Bake uncovered at 350 degrees for 30 minutes.

Yield: 8 servings

STUFFED BELL PEPPERS

10 large bell peppers
1 pound of lean ground pork or beef
1 large onion, chopped
1 eggplant, peeled and pureed
Salt, black pepper and cayenne pepper, to taste
¼ cup of chopped parsley
¼ cup of chopped green onion tops
Bread crumbs

1. Cut 8 of the bell peppers in half, crosswise, and remove the stems and seeds; chop remaining bell peppers.
2. Brown the meat and add 1 chopped bell pepper and onion; cook until the onions are transparent.
3. Add eggplant and simmer for about 5 minutes; season with salt, black pepper and cayenne pepper and remove from heat.
4. Add the remaining chopped bell pepper, parsley and green onion tops; stuff mixture into bell pepper halves and sprinkle with bread crumbs. (If mixture is rather loose add bread crumbs to stiffen before stuffing.)
5. Place stuffed bell peppers into a shallow baking pan and add a small amount of water to the bottom of the pan; bake at 350 degrees for 30 minutes or until the tops become crusty and brown.

Yield: 16 servings

Note: These freeze very well. To freeze, blanch bell pepper halves in boiling water for three minutes; drain and stuff as above.

CABBAGE ROLLS

1 large cabbage
2 pounds of lean ground chuck
1 large onion, chopped
1 bell pepper, chopped
4 stalks of celery, chopped
½ cup of raw rice
2 10-ounce cans of tomatoes with chilies
3 8-ounce cans of tomato sauce
Salt, black pepper and cayenne pepper, to taste

1. Place cabbage in boiling water for 5 minutes; remove large leaves and reserve.
2. Mix remaining ingredients, using one-half of the tomatoes and tomato sauce.
3. Place rounded tablespoons of the mixture in each leaf; roll up, tucking edges in as you roll.
4. Place in a large, heavy pot and pour remaining tomatoes and tomato sauce over rolls; sprinkle with a little more salt and cayenne pepper.
5. Cover pot tightly and steam for about 1 to 1½ hours over medium-low heat.

Yield: 8 servings

GRILLADE PANNE
Breaded Veal

1 pound of veal or beef round (center cut), about ½ inch thick
Salt and cayenne pepper, to taste
2 eggs, well beaten
¼ bell pepper, chopped
Corn meal or bread crumbs
Oil for frying
Tomato Gravy (Recipe follows)

1. Cut round steak into strips about 3 inches long; season with salt and cayenne pepper.
2. Combine eggs and bell pepper; soak meat in egg mixture for about one hour.
3. Dip each piece of meat into corn meal or bread crumbs and fry in hot oil at 375 degrees until golden brown.
4. Serve with Tomato Gravy.

Tomato Gravy

2 tablespoons of flour
2 tablespoons of oil
1 onion, chopped
2 cloves of garlic, minced
½ bell pepper, chopped
1 16-ounce can of whole tomatoes, chopped
1 cup of water
Salt and cayenne pepper, to taste
Pinch of sugar

1. Make a light brown roux with flour and oil; add onion, garlic and bell pepper and cook until onions are transparent.
2. Add tomatoes and continue to cook until oil rises to the top, about 20 to 30 minutes; add water, salt, cayenne pepper and sugar and simmer about 30 minutes.

Yield: 4 servings

GRILLADES
Steaks Acadian

1 pound of round steak
Salt and cayenne pepper, to taste
½ cup of oil
1 large onion, thinly sliced
1 large bell pepper, chopped
Hot pepper sauce, to taste

1. Cut round steaks into serving pieces and season with salt and cayenne pepper.
2. Add steaks to hot oil in a heavy skillet to brown. Do not turn over until you can see brown from the sides. Then turn over and brown the other side.
3. Add onion and bell pepper, cover tightly and lower heat; simmer about 45 minutes or until meat is tender.
4. Add hot pepper sauce and serve over cooked rice or grits.

Yield: 4 servings

BOEUF ROTI
Roast Beef

5-pound round roast
2 cloves of garlic, sliced
Salt, black pepper, cayenne pepper and garlic powder to taste
Oil
2 onions, chopped
1 bell pepper, chopped
3 ribs celery, chopped

1. Insert slices of garlic into roast; season roast with salt, black pepper, cayenne pepper and garlic powder and refrigerate for two days.
2. Heat oil in a heavy pot and add roast, browning both sides; cover pot and cook on a very low heat for 8 hours.
3. During the last 30 minutes of cooking, add onion and bell pepper and celery.

Yield: 8 servings

SMOTHERED ROUND STEAK IN ONIONS

3 pounds of round steak, ½ inch thick
2 tablespoons of vinegar
1 tablespoon of salt
1 teaspoon of black pepper
½ teaspoon of cayenne pepper
Flour
3 tablespoons of oil
¾ cup of water
1 large onion, sliced thin

1. Pound steak to tenderize and thin it slightly; pour vinegar over steak and season with salt, black pepper and cayenne pepper.
2. Dredge steak with flour and brown in hot oil on medium heat on both sides in a covered skillet; add ½ cup of the water, cover and simmer about 30 to 45 minutes.
3. Remove steak from skillet, add onions and cook until onions are brown; add remaining ¼ cup of water and return steak to skillet.
4. Cover and continue to simmer for 30 minutes; serve over cooked rice.

Yield: 6 to 8 servings

BOEUF A LA MODE

1 pound of round steak, ½-inch thick
Salt, black pepper and cayenne pepper, to taste
6 large carrots, peeled and cut lengthwise into thin strips
½ pound of bacon
½ cup of oil
2 onions, chopped
1 bell pepper, chopped
3 stalks of celery, chopped
2 teaspoons of garlic powder
6 to 8 potatoes, peeled and cut into bite-size pieces
1 cup of water

1. Pound steak and season to taste with salt, black pepper and cayenne pepper.
2. Place carrots and bacon slices on steak; roll up steak in jellyroll-fashion and tie securely.
3. Brown steak roll in oil until brown on all sides; add onions, bell pepper, celery and garlic powder and saute until onions are transparent.
4. Add potatoes and water, cover and slowly cook until steak is tender, about one hour.

Yield: 4 servings

BRISKET STUFFED WITH CORNBREAD DRESSING

1 6-pound beef brisket
Salt, black pepper and cayenne pepper, to taste
Cornbread Dressing (Recipe follows)

1. Open pocket in the brisket from the thin side. (Be careful not to pierce the two ends, the top or the bottom.)
2. Season with salt, black pepper and cayenne pepper.
3. Fill pocket in the brisket with Cornbread Dressing. Using a large needle and cotton string, sew the open side of the brisket; place in a covered roast pan.
4. Cook at 350 degrees for two hours, basting occasionally.

Yield: 10 to 12 servings

Cornbread Dressing

6 tablespoons of flour
¼ cup of oil
1 pound of ground beef
1 pound of ground pork
1 cup of chopped onions
½ cup of chopped bell peppers
½ cup of chopped celery
½ cup of chopped green onions
¼ cup of finely minced parsley
1 clove of garlic, finely chopped
1 cup of finely chopped pecans
1 2-cup recipe of cornbread,
  prepared and baked

1. Make a roux of the flour and oil in a small skillet.
2. Brown the beef and pork together in a large heavy pot; add vegetables.
3. When vegetables become limp, add roux and enough water to make a thick gravy; cook on a low heat for one hour.
4. Stir in pecans; simmer for ten minutes; remove from heat.
5. Crumble cornbread into dressing stock; mix well.

DAUBE GLACE

4 to 5 pounds veal or beef round roast
1 bell pepper, chopped
3 cloves of garlic, minced
Salt and cayenne pepper, to taste
4 calf knuckles
1 envelope of unflavored gelatin
4 boiled eggs, sliced
½ cup of olives, sliced
¼ cup of chopped pimento

1. Make slits in the roast and stuff with a mixture of bell pepper, garlic, salt and cayenne pepper; brown in a heavy pot in a small amount of oil.
2. Lower heat, cover pot and continue to cook for 2 to 3 hours or until roast is tender and falling apart. A small amount of water can be added from time to time to keep roast from sticking.
3. In a separate pot, boil calf knuckles in water to cover until tender and the meat falls off bone, about one hour.
4. Dissolve gelatin and add to broth of calf knuckles; season with salt and cayenne pepper.
5. Grease a round bottom glass dish and place sliced eggs, olives and pimento on bottom and sides of the dish; spoon a little gelatin mixture over this and let it set.
6. Slice or pull cooked roast apart and place on top of eggs and olives; pour remaining gelatin over roast so that all of the meat is covered.
7. Refrigerate overnight; unmold to serve; serve sliced as you would a cold cut.

CALF LIVER IN WINE

1 pound of calf liver, cut into serving pieces
1 cup of flour
2 tablespoons of butter
1 onion, chopped
½ cup of white wine
Salt, black pepper and cayenne pepper, to taste

1. Dredge liver in flour and saute in butter over medium heat just long enough for some of the flour to stick to the bottom of the pot.
2. Remove liver from pot; add onions and cook until transparent. (You may have to add some more butter.)
3. Add liver and wine and simmer 5 to 10 minutes; season with salt, black pepper and cayenne pepper and serve over cooked rice.

Yield: 4 servings

SMOTHERED LIVER

1 pound of calf liver
3 tablespoons of oil
Salt, black pepper and cayenne pepper, to taste
2 large onions, sliced
½ cup of water

1. Brown liver in oil over high heat, turning only once.
2. Add salt, black pepper, cayenne pepper, onion rings and water; cook about 5 to 6 minutes.
3. Serve over grits.

Yield: 4 servings

KIDNEY STEW

2 beef or veal kidneys
½ cup of flour
½ cup of oil
2 large onions, chopped
1 large bell pepper, chopped
4 stalks of celery, chopped
1 cup of water
Salt, black pepper and cayenne pepper, to taste
1 fresh jalapeno pepper, chopped
½ cup of chopped green onion tops
½ cup of chopped parsley
1 to 2 tablespoons of claret wine (optional)

1. Boil kidneys 15 minutes in water to cover; rinse in cold water.
2. Peel skin off of each lobe; cut into bite-size pieces.
3. Make a light brown roux with flour and oil; add onion, bell pepper and celery and cook until onions are transparent.
4. Add water, salt, black pepper, cayenne pepper, jalapeno pepper and kidneys; simmer about 30 minutes.
5. Add green onion tops and parsley; add claret if desired.

Yield: 4 servings

TONGUE A L'ACADIEN

1 fresh beef tongue, washed thoroughly
¼ cup of oil
2 onions, chopped
1 bell pepper, cut into strips
4 cloves of garlic, minced
2 stalks of celery, chopped
1½ cups of water
Salt, black pepper and cayenne pepper to taste

1. Cover tongue with boiling water and cook until tender, about 1½ hours; plunge into cold water and let stand about 5 minutes.
2. Remove from water and skin tongue.
3. Brown tongue in oil slowly; add onions, bell pepper, garlic and celery and cook until onions are transparent.
4. Add water, salt, black pepper and cayenne pepper and simmer in a covered pot about one hour over low heat.
5. Slice into thin slices to serve.

Yield: 4 to 6 servings

LAGNIAPPE STEW

2 beef kidneys
1 beef brain
1 beef heart
1 pound of beef liver
Marrow guts from one calf
Salt and cayenne pepper to taste
1 cup of flour
1 cup of oil
3 medium onions, chopped
1 bell pepper, chopped
4 stalks of celery, chopped
2 teaspoons of garlic powder
2 pounds of fresh pork sausage, removed from casing (See
    page 96)
¼ cup of chopped parsley
¼ cup of chopped green onion tops

1. Cover kidneys with water and boil 15 minutes; remove from heat and drain.
2. Run hot tap water over brain and peel off skin.
3. Cut kidney, brain, heart, liver and marrow guts into bite-size pieces and season highly with salt and cayenne pepper.
3. Make a dark brown roux with flour and oil; add onions, bell pepper, and celery and cook until onions are transparent.
4. Add kidneys, heart, liver, marrow guts, garlic powder and pork sausage to roux mixture; cover with water and simmer for about 3 hours in a covered pot.
5. Add brain and continue to cook for 10 minutes; add parsley and green onion tops.

Yield: 15 to 20 servings

CAJUN PORK PATE

1 pound of pork liver, ¼ inch thick
1 onion, chopped
2 tablespoons of oil
2 pounds of pork loin, cut into chunks
1 whole nutmeg, grated
1 tablespoon of salt
1 tablespoon of black pepper
1 teaspoon of cayenne pepper
3 pounds of pork fat
2 bay leaves

1. Brown liver and onions in oil until liver is whitish and no blood shows.
2. Grind liver, onions and pork loin in a food processor or food grinder; add the drippings from the pan in which the liver was cooked, nutmeg, salt, black pepper and cayenne pepper and mix well.
3. Cut 1 pound of the pork fat into ½-inch cubes and boil in water with the bay leaves for three minutes; drain and cool.
4. Mix pork fat with pork meat thoroughly, using your hands and blending fat into the meat and liver.
5. Cut the remaining pork fat into thin strips about 2 inches wide; line the bottom and sides of a heavy baking dish or loaf pan with these strips.
6. Place the pork meat mixture into baking dish and cover top with more slices of fat, making sure the pate is well covered with fat; place bay leaves on top and cover baking dish with a lid or heavy foil.
7. Bake at 350 degrees for one hour and 15 minutes; fat should be well browned; if not remove cover and bake uncovered until brown.
8. Cool at least 5 to 6 hours before removing from baking dish; keep fat on pate unti it is served, then remove the fat.

Note: This will keep for about 2 weeks with the fat layers on it. Serve with crackers or on open face sandwiches.

ANDOUILLE

5 pounds of pork stomach (maws)
10 pounds of pork butt, cut into ½-inch cubes
½ pound of fresh garlic, minced
1 ounce of cayenne pepper
½ ounce of black pepper
½ cup of curing salt
¼ cup of monosodium glutamate
Sausage casing

1. Rinse pork stomach in salty water, cut open and remove all fat; grind coarsely in food processor or food grinder.
2. Mix all ingredients together and stuff into casing using a funnel or sausage stuffer.

Yield: 15 pounds of fresh andouille
Use in gumbos.

Note: If a smoker is available smoke at 120 degrees to 150 degrees for approximately 4 to 6 hours.

PORK SAUSAGE

4 pounds of lean ground pork
2 pounds of ground pork fat
1 tablespoon of salt
2 teaspoons of black pepper
2 teaspoons of cayenne pepper
2 large onions, chopped fine
6 cloves of garlic, minced
1 bunch of green onion tops, chopped fine
Sausage casing, scalded

1. Combine ingredients, except casing and mix well.
2. Fill sausage casing using a funnel or sausage stuffer, tying the ends.

Yield: About 6 pounds of fresh pork sausage
Note: High seasoning is the characteristic of pork sausage.
Instead of stuffing into casing, sausage can be shaped into patties or packaged in bulk to use in recipes calling for "sausage removed from casing."

SMOTHERED PORK SAUSAGE

2 pounds of fresh pork sausage (See above recipe)
2 tablespoons of oil
1 onion, chopped
¼ bell pepper, chopped

1. Brown sausage in oil in a heavy skillet on medium heat; add onions and bell pepper.
2. Lower heat, add ¼ cup of water, cover skillet and continue to cook for 30 to 45 minutes. Add water, ¼ cup at a time, as it cooks down.
3. Remove sausage from skillet; add 1 cup of water, bring to a boil and cook on medium heat about 10 minutes or until gravy thickens.
4. Serve over cooked rice.

Yield: 4 to 6 servings

STUFFED EGGPLANT

3 eggplants
1 onion, chopped
½ pound of ground pork
Salt, black pepper and cayenne pepper, to taste
¼ cup of flour
½ cup of oil
½ cup of water
¼ cup of chopped green onion tops
¼ cup of chopped parsley
4 to 5 slices of toasted bread, torn into small pieces
Bread crumbs

1. Cut each eggplant in half and scoop out the center with a spoon, leaving a shell with sides about ½-inch thick.
2. Cook the eggplant pulp until it is soft; add onion, pork, salt, black pepper and cayenne pepper and continue to cook until the pork is brown and the onions are transparent.
3. Make a light brown roux with the flour and oil; add water, stir until roux is dissolved; add the eggplant mixture and continue to cook about 20 minutes.
4. Add green onion tops and parsley and cook about 5 minutes; add the toasted bread and mix well.
5. Butter the inside of each eggplant shell and fill with pork stuffing; sprinkle with bread crumbs and bake at 400 degrees until brown, about 20 minutes.

Yield: 6 servings

PORK WITH TURNIPS

3 pounds of pork chops, about ½ inch thick
Salt, black pepper and cayenne pepper, to taste
½ cup of oil
½ cup of flour
1 large onion, chopped
1 large bell pepper, chopped
1 tablespoon of minced garlic
3 to 4 cups of water
8 medium-size turnips, peeled and chopped

1. Season pork with salt, black pepper and cayenne pepper and brown in oil.
2. Remove pork and add flour to oil in pot and make a dark brown roux; add onion, bell pepper and garlic and cook until onions are transparent.
3. Add pork and water; bring to a boil; lower heat and simmer until meat is tender, about 45 minutes.
4. Add turnips and continue cooking for about 20 to 30 minutes.

Yield: 6 to 8 servings

PORK ROAST

½ **bell pepper, chopped**
4 cloves of garlic, minced
1 onion, chopped
1 cup of chopped celery
Salt and cayenne pepper, to taste
4 pound pork roast
¼ **cup of oil**
2 cups of water

1. Combine bell pepper, garlic, onion, celery, salt and cayenne pepper; make slits in the pork roast and stuff the onion mixture into the slits.
2. Rub the remaining onion mixture on the outside of the roast.
3. Brown roast on all sides in the oil; add water, cover pot and cook on low heat about 3½ hours or until roast is tender.

Yield: 6 to 8 servings

PORK GRILLADE

12 pork chops
Salt, black pepper and cayenne pepper to taste
4 onions
Vinegar
Oil
1 bell pepper, chopped
½ stalk of celery, chopped
6 cloves of garlic, chopped
¾ cup of water

1. Season pork chops with salt, black pepper and cayenne; add 2 sliced onions and cover with vinegar. Refrigerate pork chops for two to three days.
2. Remove pork chops from marinade and brown over medium heat in enough oil to cover the bottom of the pan; add 2 chopped onions, bell pepper, celery and garlic and cook until onions are transparent.
3. Add water, cover and simmer about 45 minutes or until pork chops are tender; serve over cooked rice or grits.
Yield: 6 servings

Note: It may be necessary to add more water as pork chops cook to make a gravy.

FRIED PORK CHOPS

4 pork chops, ¼-inch thick
Salt, black pepper, cayenne pepper and garlic powder, to taste
Flour
Oil for frying

1. Season pork chops with salt, black pepper, cayenne pepper and garlic powder; dredge both sides in flour, coating thoroughly.
2. Deep fry in hot oil at 350 degrees until golden brown, about 10 minutes.

Yield: 4 servings

PORK FRICASSEE

1½ cups of flour
1½ cups of oil
2 onions, chopped
1 large bell pepper, chopped
4 stalks of celery, chopped
6 cloves of garlic, minced
12 large pork chops (pork backbone can be also used)
Salt, black pepper and cayenne pepper, to taste

1. Make a light brown roux with flour and oil; add onions, bell pepper, celery and garlic and cook until onions are transparent.
2. Add pork and enough water to cover one layer of meat; simmer for about one hour or until gravy is thick and pork is tender.

Yield: 12 servings

PORK CHOPS IN TOMATO GRAVY

6 pork chops, about ½ inch thick
Salt and cayenne pepper, to taste
2 cups of tomato juice
Hot pepper sauce
1 teaspoon of lemon juice
¼ bell pepper, chopped
1 onion, chopped
1 teaspoon of basil
1 bay leaf

1. Season pork chops with salt and cayenne pepper; brown in a heavy skillet.
2. Add remaining ingredients, bring to a boil; lower heat, cover and cook slowly for about 30 minutes or until pork chops are tender.
3. Serve with cooked rice.

Yield: 6 servings

HOGSHEAD CHEESE

1 hog's head, cut into pieces with eyes, ears and snout removed
4 pounds of pork butt, cut into pieces
6 to 8 hog's feet
2 large onions, chopped
1 large bell pepper, chopped
3 tablespoons of minced garlic
½ cup of chopped parsley
½ cup of chopped green onion tops
Salt, black pepper and cayenne pepper, to taste

1. Place head, pork butt, feet, onions and bell pepper in a large pot. Cover with water and boil about 3 hours or until tender.
2. Remove hog's head, pork butt and feet. Cool then remove skin, bones and fat. Grind meat in food processor or grinder. To this meat add enough of the broth to soften it up.
3. Add parsley, onion tops, salt, black pepper and cayenne pepper; pour into a large glass baking dish and refrigerate overnight. (Mixture will gel.)
4. To serve, unmold from baking dish and slice; serve with crackers or French bread.

CRACKLINS
Gratons

1 quart of hog lard
10 pounds of pork fat with skin, cut into 1-inch pieces
Salt, to taste

1. Heat hog lard in a large, heavy pot; add pork fat pieces, stirring often to prevent sticking.
2. When cracklins start to float in oil and are getting brown, remove with a slotted spoon and drain on paper towels.
3. While still hot, add salt to taste.

Note: These are better served fresh; however, to keep for a short period of time, seal in tightly-covered container.

CHITTERLINGS
Small Intestines of Pig

2 pounds of chitterlings
1 teaspoon of minced garlic
1 fresh cayenne pepper, chopped (or ground cayenne pepper,
**   to taste)**
1 egg, beaten
1 tablespoon of water
Cracker crumbs
Oil for frying

1. Wash chitterlings thoroughly and cover with boiling salted water; add garlic and cayenne pepper and cook until tender, about two hours.
2. Drain chitterlings and cut into two-inch pieces; dip each piece into egg beaten with water and then into cracker crumbs.
3. Fry in hot oil at 375 degrees until brown; drain on paper towels.

Yield: 4 to 6 servings

BOUDIN

1 hog's head, cut into pieces with eyes, ears and snout removed
1½ pounds of pork liver
2 onions, cut into chunks
2 stalks of celery
1 large bell pepper, cut into chunks
4 to 6 pounds of pork butt, cut into chunks
6 pig's feet
Salt, black pepper and cayenne pepper, to taste
3 pounds of rice, cooked
1 hank of sausage casing

1. Place all ingredients except rice and sausage casing into a large pot; cover with water and boil one to two hours or until meat is tender.
2. Remove ingredients from broth and continue to cook broth until reduced by half.
3. Remove all bones and excess fat from head, feet and pork butt and grind entire mixture in food processor or grinder.
4. Season with salt, black pepper and cayenne pepper. (This dish is a highly seasoned dish.)
5. Mix with cooked rice, stirring the mixture as little as possible to prevent rice from breaking. If too dry, add some of the broth.
6. Fill the sausage casing using a funnel or sausage stuffer, tying the ends.
7. Simmer boudin in broth for 15 minutes.

Yield: 15 to 20 pounds

GIGOT DE MOUTON
Leg of Lamb

Salt, black pepper and cayenne pepper, to taste
1 onion, finely chopped
1 bell pepper, finely chopped
1 clove of garlic, minced
1 leg of lamb

1. Combine salt, black pepper, cayenne pepper, onion, bell pepper and garlic together.
2. Cut slits in lamb all over; stuff seasoning mixture into the slits and rub remaining seasoning mixture all over the leg.
3. Brown in a hot oven (450 degrees) for 20 to 30 minutes; when brown, lower heat to 350 degrees and continue to bake for 1 to 1½ hours.

Yield: 8 to 10 servings

Poultry

POULTRY

CHICKEN-OYSTER PIE

2 tablespoons of oleo
2 tablespoons of flour
1 small onion, chopped
½ stalk of celery, chopped
¼ bell pepper, chopped
1 cup of chicken broth
2 to 3 dozen oysters, coarsely chopped
1 cup of cooked chicken, chopped
Salt, black pepper and cayenne pepper, to taste
1 cup of bread crumbs
Pastry for double-crust pie

1. Make a dark brown roux with oleo and flour; add onion, celery and bell pepper; mix with roux and cook briefly.
2. Slowly add chicken broth, stirring constantly; add oysters and cook about 2 to 3 minutes.
3. Add remaining ingredients except pastry and mix well; mixture should be stiff.
4. Pour mixture into baked pie shell and top with uncooked second crust; bake at 400 degrees for about 30 to 45 minutes or until golden brown.

Yield: 6 to 8 servings

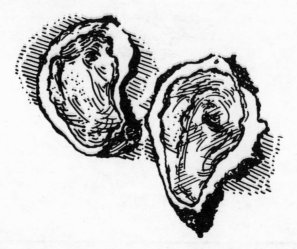

CHICKEN FRICASSEE

1 hen (4 to 5 pounds), cut into serving pieces
Salt and cayenne pepper, to taste
6 tablespoons of oil
6 tablespoons of flour
2 large onions, chopped
4 cups of hot water

1. Season hen with salt and cayenne pepper and brown in hot oil; remove hen from oil and add flour, stirring to make a dark brown roux.
2. Add onions and cook until they are transparent; return hen to pot, add water and cook on low heat for about 2 hours or until hen is tender.
3. Serve over cooked rice or debone hen and serve in patty shells.

Yield: 6 servings

EGGPLANT-CHICKEN CASSEROLE

4 to 5 eggplants, peeled and cubed
2 medium onions, chopped
¾ cup of chopped bell pepper
½ cup of green onions
2 cloves of garlic, minced
2 tablespoons of cooking oil
2 cups of chopped cooked chicken
Bread crumbs
Butter

1. Boil eggplant until tender, about 30 minutes.
2. In another pot, saute onions, bell pepper, green onions and garlic in oil; add this and chicken to boiled eggplant.
3. Put in casserole, cover with bread crumbs and dot with butter.
4. Bake uncovered at 350 degrees for 40 minutes.

Yield: 8 servings

CAJUN SMOTHERED CHICKEN

1 chicken, cut into serving pieces
Salt, black pepper and cayenne pepper, to taste
½ cup of oil
1 pound of fresh pork sausage (See page 96)
3 large onions, chopped
1 large bell pepper, chopped
4 stalks of celery, chopped
2 teaspoons of garlic powder
2 cups of water
½ cup of chopped green onion tops
½ cup of chopped parsley

1. Season chicken with salt, black pepper and cayenne pepper; brown chicken in hot oil in a large heavy skillet and remove from skillet when brown.
2. Brown pork sausage in oil, remove from skillet and cut into 1½-inch pieces.
3. Remove most of the oil from the skillet and add onion, bell pepper and celery; cook until onions are transparent.
4. Add pork sausage, chicken and garlic powder to skillet with onions; slowly add water, cover and simmer 30 to 40 minutes.
5. Add green onion tops and parsley just before serving; serve over cooked rice.

Yield: 4 servings

CHICKEN SAUTE AUX GROS ONIONS
Chicken Smothered in Onions

2 large chickens, cut into serving pieces
Salt and cayenne pepper, to taste
1 cup of oil
⅓ cup of flour
2 onions, sliced thin
1 small bell pepper, chopped

1. Season chickens with salt and cayenne pepper and brown in oil, removing pieces as they are brown to make room for the remaining chicken; sprinkle flour on chicken pieces as they are browning.
2. When all chicken is brown, return all pieces to the pot and add onions and bell pepper; cover the pot and cook on low heat about one hour or until chicken is tender, adding small amounts of water as necessary to prevent sticking.
3. When ready to serve, you might have to add a small amount of water to make a gravy; serve with cooked rice.
Yield: 8 servings

CHICKEN MAQUE CHOUX

1 chicken, cut into serving pieces
Salt, black pepper and cayenne pepper, to taste
½ cup of oil
12 ears of fresh corn, cut from the cob
2 onions, chopped
½ bell pepper, chopped
1 tomato, peeled and chopped

1. Season chicken with salt, black pepper and cayenne pepper and brown in hot oil in a heavy pot; remove from pot as it browns.
2. Add remaining ingredients, stir and cook on medium-high heat about 2 minutes; return chicken to pot, stir, cover and cook over medium heat for 30 minutes, stirring two or three times during the cooking.
3. Serve over cooked rice.

Yield: 4 to 6 servings

CHICKEN STEW

1 chicken, cut into serving pieces
Salt, black pepper and cayenne pepper, to taste
⅓ cup of flour
⅓ cup of oil
1 large onion, chopped
½ tomato, peeled and chopped
1 small bell pepper, chopped
Chicken broth

1. Season chicken with salt, black pepper and cayenne pepper; bake at 400 degrees for 20 minutes.
2. Make a dark brown roux with flour and oil; add onion and cook until onion is transparent.
3. Add tomato and bell pepper; simmer for about 15 minutes, adding small amounts of chicken broth if mixture sticks to bottom of pan.
4. Pour liquid left from baking chicken into a measuring cup and let the fat separate; pour off the fat and add the remaining liquid and the chicken to the roux mixture.
5. Mix well, partially cover pot and cook about 30 to 45 minutes, stirring occasionally.
6. Serve over cooked rice or with dumplings. (See following recipe.)

Yield: 4 servings

Note: This dish has a much better flavor if not served until 3 or 4 hours after it is cooked.

DUMPLINGS

1½ cups of sifted flour
2 teaspoons of baking powder
¾ teaspoon of salt
3 tablespoons of chopped green onion tops
1 tablespoon of chopped parsley
¾ cup of milk

1. Sift flour, baking powder and salt together; add green onion tops and parsley.
2. Add milk and stir only until well blended.
3. Drop by spoonfuls into boiling stew. Dip spoon into hot stew and then into dumpling mixture; this will make the batter slide easily off of the spoon.
4. Cook for 15 minutes in a tightly covered pot; do not remove cover.
5. Serve hot with Chicken Stew.

Yield: 6 to 8 servings

Seafood

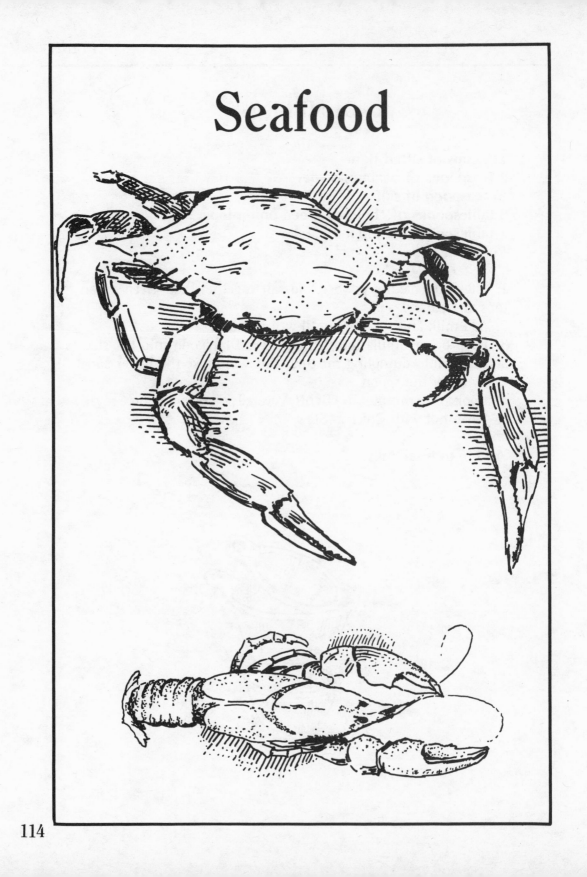

SEAFOOD

"FISH: Louisiana's southern boundary and the Gulf of Mexico is the meeting place and home of some of the finest fish. The many bayous and the Gulf provided the ingredients for many tasty Acadian dishes too numerous to name here."

BAKED STUFFED CATFISH

2 onions, chopped
4 stalks of celery, chopped
1 bell pepper, chopped
½ cup of butter
2 10-ounce cans of tomatoes with chilies
1 8-ounce can of tomato sauce
Salt, black pepper and cayenne pepper, to taste
¼ cup of chopped parsley
¼ cup of chopped green onion tops
1 5-pound whole catfish, cleaned and head removed
Shrimp and Crab Stuffing (Recipe follows)

1. Saute onion, celery and bell pepper in butter until onions are transparent; add remaining ingredients except fish and stuffing and simmer about 20 to 30 minutes.
2. Season fish with salt, black pepper and cayenne pepper and stuff cavity with Shrimp and Crab Stuffing.
3. Place stuffed fish in a foil-lined baking dish and pour tomato mixture over the top; close foil over fish tightly and bake at 350 degrees for about 30 to 45 minutes.

Yield: 4 to 6 servings

Shrimp and Crab Stuffing

1 onion, chopped
½ bell pepper, chopped
¼ cup of oil
½ pound of peeled and deveined shrimp
½ pound of crab meat
Salt, black pepper and cayenne pepper, to taste
¼ cup of water

1. Saute onion and bell pepper in oil until onions are transparent.
2. Add shrimp, crab meat, salt, black pepper, cayenne pepper and water and simmer 5 minutes.

FRIED CATFISH

1½ cups of yellow corn meal
2½ cups of flour
½ cup of chopped parsley
Salt and cayenne pepper, to taste
2 pounds of catfish filets
Oil for frying

1. Combine corn meal, flour, parsley, salt and cayenne pepper.
2. Season catfish and dip into corn meal mixture, shaking off excess flour.
3. Fry in hot, deep oil at 375 degrees until golden brown; drain on paper towels.

Yield: 4 to 6 servings

BAKED STUFFED FLOUNDER

½ pound of butter
1 pound of fresh crab meat
½ pound of shrimp, peeled and deveined
1 cup of chopped onions
½ cup of chopped parsley
½ cup of chopped green onion tops
2 teaspoons of lemon juice
¼ teaspoon of grated lemon rind
2 cups of fine bread crumbs, seasoned with salt
  and cayenne pepper
2 eggs
Salt and cayenne pepper, to taste
8 flounders
½ cup of dry white wine

1. Melt ¼ pound of the butter; add crab meat and shrimp and cook on medium heat until shrimp are pink, about 10 minutes.
2. Add onions and cook until onions are transparent; add parsley, green onion tops, 1 teaspoon of the lemon juice and lemon rind and cook another 5 minutes.
3. Remove from heat and add bread crumbs, eggs, salt and pepper and mix well.
4. Make a pocket in each flounder by cutting a slit down the center of the top of each fish; slide knife along the backbone of the fish on each side of the center to create a pocket with two flaps.
5. Season fish inside and out with salt and cayenne pepper; fill pockets with crab-shrimp stuffing and place in a large baking pan.
6. Bake uncovered at 375 degrees, basting with a mixture of ¼ pound of melted butter, 1 teaspoon of lemon juice and wine, for 20 minutes; lower heat to 300 degrees and bake another 15 to 20 minutes.

Yield: 8 servings

BAKED REDFISH

4 to 6 pound whole redfish (or red snapper)
Salt, black pepper and cayenne pepper, to taste
2 tomatoes, thinly sliced
1 large onion, thinly sliced
1 lemon, thinly sliced
¼ pound of butter, melted
Juice of 1 lemon
¼ cup of chopped parsley

1. Make 2 or 3 diagonal slashes on each side of the fish; season fish inside and out with salt, black pepper and cayenne pepper.
2. Place in a baking pan; top fish with alternate overlapping slices of tomato, onion and lemon.
3. Mix butter and lemon juice and pour over the fish; bake at 350 degrees for 10 minutes per pound of fish, basting often during the baking time.
4. Sprinkle the top with parsley and serve.

Yield: 8 to 12 servings

BROILED REDFISH

3 pounds of redfish filets
Salt and cayenne pepper, to taste
¼ pound of butter, melted
Juice of 1 lemon
6 bay leaves
1 lemon, thinly sliced

1. Season fish filets with salt and cayenne pepper; place in a heavy metal baking dish.
2. Mix melted butter and lemon juice and brush over the top of each filet; place 1 bay leaf on each filet and top with lemon slices.
3. Broil 6 inches from heat for about 10 minutes or until fish flakes with a fork; baste often during broiling with remaining butter-lemon mixture.

Yield: 6 servings

STUFFED RED SNAPPER

1 onion, chopped
½ cup of chopped celery
½ pound of butter
1 cup of peeled shrimp
1 cup of crab meat
¾ cup of bread crumbs
½ cup of chopped green onions
¾ cup of chopped parsley
Salt, black pepper and cayenne pepper, to taste
4 to 6 pound red snapper (or redfish)
Juice of 1 lemon
1 lemon, sliced

1. Saute onion and celery in ¼ pound of the butter until onions are transparent; add shrimp, crab meat, bread crumbs, green onions, and ½ cup of the parsley and mix well.
2. Season shrimp-crab mixture with salt, black pepper and cayenne pepper and mix; season fish inside and out with salt, black pepper and cayenne pepper and stuff the cavity with shrimp-crab mixture.
3. Melt remaining ¼ pound of butter and mix with the lemon juice; pour over the fish in a baking pan.
4. Bake at 350 degrees for 10 minutes per pound of fish, basting often with the butter mixture; remove from oven and top with remaining ¼ cup of parsley and lemon slices.

Yield: 8 to 12 servings

BAKED SPECKLED TROUT

2 pounds of speckled trout filets
Salt and cayenne pepper, to taste
½ pound of thinly sliced cheddar cheese
¼ cup of chopped parsley
1 teaspoon of oregano
3 cloves of garlic, minced
1 teaspoon of thyme
2 onions, chopped
¼ cup of oil
2 tablespoons of flour
1½ cups of milk

1. Season trout with salt and cayenne pepper; in a greased baking dish layer fish and cheese alternately, ending with cheese.
2. Sprinkle parsley, oregano, garlic and thyme over the top.
3. Saute onions in oil until onions are transparent; add flour, salt and cayenne pepper and stir until blended but not brown.
4. Gradually add milk, stirring constantly; cook on medium heat until mixture thickens; pour over fish.
5. Bake at 400 degrees 20 to 30 minutes or until fish flakes easily with fork.

Yield: 6 servings

CRAB STEW

½ cup of oil
½ cup of flour
2 large onions, chopped
2 stalks of celery, chopped
½ bell pepper, chopped
4 cloves of garlic, minced
2 quarts of hot water
30 fresh crabs, back shell removed
   and body cut in half
Salt and cayenne pepper, to taste
½ cup of chopped parsley
½ cup of chopped green onion tops

1. Make a dark brown roux with oil and flour; add onions, celery, bell pepper and garlic and cook until onions are transparent.
2. Add hot water and cook, stirring, until roux is dissolved; add crab pieces, salt, cayenne pepper and simmer for about one hour and twenty minutes.
3. Add parsley and green onion tops and serve over cooked rice.

Yield: 8 servings

CRAB MEAT CASSEROLE

½ cup of chopped green onions
½ cup of chopped celery
½ cup of chopped bell peppers
¼ cup of melted butter
2 tablespoons of flour
1 cup of milk
2 tablespoons of lemon juice
Salt and pepper, to taste
2 cups of crab meat
Buttered bread crumbs

1. Saute onions, celery and bell peppers in butter in a heavy saucepan.
2. Blend in flour; slowly add milk, stirring constantly; cook until thick.
3. Add lemon juice and seasonings; gently stir in crab meat.
4. Place in greased casserole; top with bread crumbs.
5. Bake uncovered at 350 degrees for about 20 minutes.

Yield: 4 servings

Note: Grated cheese may be substituted for bread crumbs for a quick au gratin variation.

CRAB MEAT AU GRATIN

⅓ cup of chopped green onions
½ cup of finely chopped celery
¼ cup of chopped bell pepper
½ cup of oleo
6 tablespoons of flour
1 5⅓-ounce can of evaporated milk
2 egg yolks, well-beaten
¼ cup of grated American cheese
¼ teaspoon of salt
¼ teaspoon of black pepper
Dash of red pepper
2½ to 3 cups of white lump crab meat
¼ cup of minced parsley
Grated cheese
Paprika

1. Saute vegetables in oleo, using a heavy skillet; slowly stir in flour; then slowly stir in milk and egg yolks.
2. Add one-fourth cup of cheese; let melt over low heat, stirring often.
3. Add seasonings; carefully stir in crab meat; add parsley.
4. Put mixture into six buttered individual clam shells (three to four inches) or into a casserole. Sprinkle tops with a little grated cheese and paprika.
5. Bake uncovered at 350 degrees until hot and bubbly and top is delicately browned.

Yield: 6 servings

FRIED SOFT-SHELL CRABS

8 soft-shell crabs
2 eggs, beaten
¼ cup of water
Salt and cayenne pepper, to taste
Bread crumbs or flour
Oil for frying

1. To clean soft-shell crabs: remove apron from under the body, lift up each point of the shell and remove the spongy substance; then cut off the eyes and the sand bag between the eyes and wash in cold water.
2. Combine eggs and water; season crabs with salt and cayenne pepper and dip each crab into the egg mixture and roll in bread crumbs or flour, coating thoroughly.
3. Fry in deep oil at 350 degrees until golden brown, about 6 minutes; drain on paper towels.

Yield: 4 servings

BROILED SOFT-SHELL CRABS

8 soft-shell crabs
Milk
1½ tablespoons of oil
½ teaspoon of salt
¼ teaspoon of cayenne pepper
8 thin slices of toast
½ cup of melted butter
¼ cup of chopped parsley
2 lemons, thinly sliced

1. To clean soft-shell crabs, see recipe for "Fried Soft-Shell Crabs."
2. Soak crabs in milk for 20 minutes; mix oil, salt and cayenne pepper together and brush each crab with this mixture.
3. Broil 6 inches from heat 10 to 15 minutes or until brown.
4. To serve, place each crab on a piece of toast, pour over butter, sprinkle with parsley and top with lemon slices.

Yield: 4 servings

STUFFED CRABS

¼ cup of flour
¼ cup of oil
1 large onion, chopped
½ large bell pepper, chopped
18 large boiled crabs, meat removed (or 2 pounds of crab meat)
6 slices of bread
1 tablespoon of finely chopped parsley
Salt, black pepper and cayenne pepper to taste
Bread crumbs

1. Make a light brown roux with flour and oil; add onions and bell peppers and cook until onions are transparent.
2. Add enough water to keep from sticking and cook for at least 20 to 30 minutes.
3. Add crab meat and cook for 15 minutes.
4. Coarsely crumb the 6 slices of bread in the food processor and add to the crab mixture with the parsley; mix well.
5. Season with salt, black pepper and cayenne pepper and stuff mixture into cleaned crab shells; sprinkle with bread crumbs.
6. Place on baking pan and bake at 350 degrees until a slight crust forms on top, about 15 to 20 minutes.

Yield: 8 servings

Note: If crab shells are not available, you may use ramekins or bake in a casserole dish.

SEAFOOD STUFFED CRABS

1 cup of chopped onions
1 cup of chopped celery
¼ cup of chopped bell pepper
¼ cup of butter or oleo
Salt, black pepper and cayenne pepper, to taste
½ cup of chicken broth
12 slices of day-old bread, toasted
1 pound of crab meat
1 cup of cooked shrimp, peeled and chopped
2 eggs, beaten
½ cup of chopped green onion tops
½ cup of chopped parsley
Bread crumbs

1. Saute onion, celery and bell pepper in butter until vegetables are transparent; add salt, black pepper, cayenne pepper and chicken broth and simmer for 20 minutes.
2. Chop bread slices in food processor or blender and add to vegetable mixture; add crab meat and shrimp, mixing with a fork, and remove from heat.
3. Cool slightly and gradually add eggs, stirring until eggs are absorbed; add green onion tops and parsley.
4. Stuff mixture into cleaned crab shells or ramekins; sprinkle with bread crumbs and dot with butter.
5. Bake at 350 degrees for 20 minutes or until brown and crusty on top.

Yield: 4 to 6 servings

CRAB-STUFFED TOMATOES

5 firm tomatoes
½ cup of sliced mushrooms
½ cup of minced onions
½ cup of chopped bell peppers
½ cup of butter
1 cup of bread crumbs
¼ cup of Parmesan cheese
½ pound of fresh crab meat
Salt, black pepper and cayenne pepper, to taste

1. Cut tomatoes in half crosswise; scoop out pulp and reserve.
2. Saute mushrooms, onions and bell peppers in butter.
3. Add bread crumbs, cheese and crab meat; season to taste.
4. Add one-half cup of reserved tomato pulp; mix well.
5. Heap mixture into tomato shells; place in greased shallow dish.
6. Bake uncovered at 350 degrees for 20 to 25 minutes or until tomatoes are heated thoroughly.

Yield: 10 servings

BOILED CRABS

3 gallons of water
2 ounces of cayenne pepper
1 pound of salt
5 dozen live crabs

1. Bring water to a boil with cayenne pepper and salt; add crabs, cover and bring back to a boil.
2. When steam appears from the edge of lid, start timing and cook 10 minutes.

Yield: 5 to 6 servings

BOILED CRAWFISH

6 gallons of water
1 large onion, quartered
2 lemons, cut in half
14 pounds of live crawfish (washed and cleaned)
½ box of salt
8 ounces of cayenne pepper

1. Bring water to a boil in a large 10-gallon pot with onions and lemons.
2. Add crawfish, cover pot and bring to a boil again; cook 5 to 7 minutes after water reaches second boil.
3. Remove crawfish and sprinkle salt and cayenne pepper over boiled crawfish.

Yield: Serves about 3 people

Note: Corn on the cob and potatoes (unpeeled) may be added just before adding crawfish.

CRAWFISH STEW

¼ **cup of oil**
¼ **cup of flour**
1 onion, chopped
1 stalk of celery, chopped
¼ **bell pepper, chopped**
1 clove of garlic, minced
1 pound of crawfish tails with fat
Salt and cayenne pepper, to taste
½ **cup of chopped parsley**
½ **cup of chopped green onion tops**

1. Make a dark brown roux with oil and flour; add onion, celery, bell pepper and garlic and cook until onions are transparent.
2. Add crawfish tails with fat (if fat is not available, simply omit it), salt and cayenne pepper; cook on low heat for 20 minutes or until fat starts to rise to the top.
3. Add parsley and green onion tops and serve over cooked rice. If gravy is too thick, add a small amount of water to reach desired consistency.

Yield: 4 to 6 servings

CRAWFISH PIE

½ cup of butter
2 tablespoons of flour
2 medium onions, chopped
½ bell pepper, chopped
2 pounds of peeled crawfish tails with the fat
½ cup of chopped green onion tops
½ cup of chopped parsley
Salt, black pepper and cayenne pepper, to taste
¼ cup of butter
1 baked pie shell

1. Make a light brown roux with butter and flour; add onion and bell pepper and cook until onions are transparent.
2. Add crawfish fat (if available) and cook 10 minutes; add crawfish tails and green onion tops and cook about 20 minutes. It may be necessary to add a little water if mixture starts to stick to bottom of pot.
3. Add parsley, salt, black pepper and cayenne pepper; pour into baked pie shell and bake at 350 degrees for 20 minutes.

Yield: 6 to 8 servings

Note: If crawfish fat is not available, simply omit it and proceed with the remainder of the recipe.

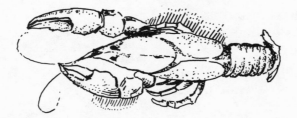

CRAWFISH AND RICE CROQUETTES

1½ pounds of crawfish tails, ground
1 cup of cooked rice
1 onion, chopped
4 cloves of garlic, chopped
1 teaspoon of minced parsley
Salt, black pepper and cayenne pepper, to taste
¾ cup of White Sauce (Recipe follows)
1 egg
1 tablespoon of water
Bread crumbs
Oil for frying

1. Mix all ingredients except egg, water, bread crumbs and oil.
2. Shape into croquettes about the size of an egg; dip in egg beaten with water.
3. Roll in bread crumbs; fry in hot oil at 375 degrees until brown and drain on paper towels.

Yield: 6 to 8 servings

White Sauce

1½ tablespoons of butter
2 tablespoons of flour
¾ cup of milk
¼ teaspoon of salt
¼ teaspoon of cayenne pepper

1. Melt butter; add flour and mix well. Do not brown.
2. Add milk slowly and cook on low heat until thick, stirring constantly.
3. Remove from heat and add salt and cayenne pepper.

BATTER FRIED CRAWFISH TAILS

1 egg, beaten
¼ cup of evaporated milk
½ teaspoon of prepared mustard
¾ teaspoon of salt
¼ teaspoon of black pepper
¼ teaspoon of garlic powder
1 cup of flour
½ cup of corn meal
½ teaspoon of baking powder
1 pound of large, peeled crawfish tails
Oil for frying

1. In a bowl, beat egg; add milk, mustard, salt, pepper and garlic powder and mix well.
2. In another bowl, sift flour, corn meal and baking powder together and stir well.
3. Dip crawfish tails into the egg mixture one at a time; drain a little and dip into the flour mixture.
4. Drop in hot oil at 375 degrees and fry until golden brown; drain on paper towels.

Yield: 4 servings

FRIED CRAWFISH

2 pounds of peeled crawfish tails
Salt, black pepper and cayenne pepper, to taste
1 egg
1 cup of milk
Bread crumbs
Oil for frying

1. Season crawfish tails with salt, black pepper and cayenne pepper.
2. Beat egg and milk together; dip crawfish into this mixture and then roll in bread crumbs.
3. Fry in deep, hot oil at 375 degrees until golden brown; drain on paper towels.

Yield: 6 servings

CRAWFISH ETOUFFEE

¼ **cup of chopped onions**
¼ **cup of chopped celery**
½ **cup of butter**
2 **pounds of peeled crawfish tails with fat**
¼ **cup of water**
Salt and cayenne pepper, to taste
¼ **cup of chopped parsley**
¼ **cup of chopped green onion tops**

1. Saute onions and celery in butter until onions are transparent; add crawfish fat and simmer 20 minutes. If crawfish fat is not available, add ¼ cup of butter.
2. Add water, salt, cayenne pepper and crawfish and simmer for 15 minutes.
3. Add parsley and green onions tops and serve over cooked rice.

Yield: 6 to 8 servings

SHRIMP STEW

½ cup of oil
½ cup of flour
1 large onion, chopped
3 cloves of garlic, minced
2 pounds of peeled and deveined shrimp
1 to 2 cups of water
Salt, black pepper and cayenne pepper, to taste
¼ cup of chopped parsley
¼ cup of chopped green onion tops

1. Make a dark brown roux with oil and flour; add onions and garlic and cook until onions are transparent.
2. Add shrimp, lower heat, cover pot and simmer for 5 to 6 minutes; add 1 cup of water and simmer for 30 minutes. If stew is too thick, add more water.
3. Add parsley and green onion tops and serve over cooked rice.

Yield: 6 to 8 servings

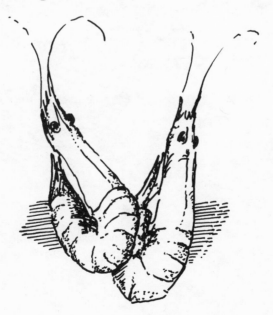

BOILED SHRIMP

1 gallon of water
1 lemon, sliced thin
1 onion, sliced
¼ cup of cayenne pepper
3 pounds of shrimp (leave peelings on)
1 cup of salt

1. Bring water, lemons, onion and cayenne pepper to a boil in a large pot; simmer for 5 to 10 minutes.

2. Add shrimp, bring to a boil and boil for 3 minutes only.

3. Remove from heat and add 1 cup of cold water (to stop the boiling process) and salt to pot of shrimp; let stand for 5 minutes and drain.

Yield: 4 to 6 servings

SHRIMP ACADIAN

1 pound of butter
1 pound of oleo
1 teaspoon of ground rosemary
3 tablespoons of black pepper
1 teaspoon of hot pepper sauce
4 lemons, sliced
4 teaspoons of salt
3 cloves of garlic, minced
8 to 10 pounds of large shrimp, unpeeled and with heads on

1. Melt butter and oleo in saucepan; add rosemary, pepper, hot sauce, lemons, salt and garlic; mix well.
2. Divide shrimp between two large shallow pans; pour an equal amount of sauce over each; stir well until shrimp are well-coated.
3. Cook at 400 degrees for 15 to 20 minutes, turning once. Shells will be pink and the meat white.

Yield: 8 servings

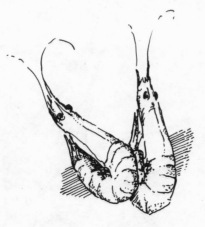

BAKED SHRIMP

3 pounds of large shrimp, peeled and deveined
1½ cups of melted butter
3 tablespoons of minced garlic
½ cup of coarsely ground black pepper
1 cup of white wine

1. Put all ingredients into a large baking dish and marinate for one hour.
2. Bake at 375 degrees until shrimp turn red, about 10 minutes; turn shrimp over and continue baking until the other side is red, about 10 minutes.
3. Serve with hot French bread.

Yield: 6 servings

Note: Much to your amazement you will have the black pepper taste but not the hot taste.

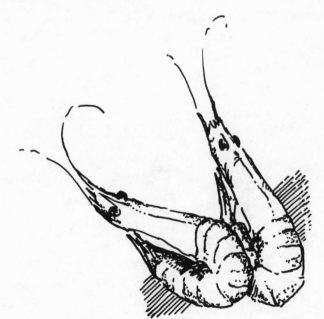

SHRIMP STUFFED MIRLITONS

4 whole mirlitons
1 onion, chopped
1 clove of garlic, minced
½ pound of peeled shrimp (or ham or ground beef)
3 tablespoons of butter
1 cup of soft bread crumbs
Salt, black pepper and cayenne pepper, to taste
1 egg
¼ cup of chopped parsley
1 teaspoon of thyme
Buttered bread crumbs

1. Boil mirlitons in salted water to cover until tender, about 45 minutes; drain, cut in half and remove the seeds.
2. Using a spoon, scoop out the pulp of the mirlitons and leave a shell about ¼ inch thick; reserve the pulp.
3. Saute onions, garlic and shrimp (or ham or beef) until shrimp are pink, about 10 minutes. (Cook beef until brown.)
4. Add soft bread crumbs, mirliton pulp, salt, black pepper and cayenne pepper and continue to cook about 5 minutes; cool slightly and add egg, parsley and thyme.
5. Stuff shrimp mixture into the mirliton shells and sprinkle the tops with buttered bread crumbs; bake at 375 degrees for 25 minutes.

Yield: 8 servings

SHRIMP-STUFFED BELL PEPPERS

½ cup of chopped onions
¼ cup of chopped celery
2 tablespoons of butter
Salt, black pepper and cayenne pepper, to taste
½ cup of tomato sauce
2 cups of cooked rice
6 medium bell peppers
¼ cup of bread crumbs
1½ pounds of shrimp, cooked, peeled and chopped (save 6
   for garnish)

1. Saute onions and celery in butter until onions are transparent; add salt, black pepper, cayenne pepper, and tomato sauce and simmer for about 6 minutes.
2. Add rice and shrimp and mix thoroughly.
3. Cut a thin slice from stem-end of bell peppers and remove seeds; drop shells into boiling water for 5 minutes and drain.
4. Fill bell peppers with shrimp stuffing and sprinkle top with bread crumbs; bake at 350 degrees for 30 minutes in a covered baking dish; uncover and bake another 10 minutes.

Yield: 6 servings

SHRIMP AU GRATIN

¾ cup of butter
¾ cup of flour
4 cups of milk
1 teaspoon of salt
1 teaspoon of pepper
1 pound of American or cheddar cheese, grated
2 cups of cooked shrimp, chopped
1 tablespoon of minced onion
Dash of hot sauce

1. Melt butter, stir in flour, and add milk, salt and pepper to make white sauce.
2. Bring mixture to a boil and add grated cheese, shrimp, onion, and hot sauce.
3. Bake in individual ramekins at 350 degrees for 30 minutes.

Yield: 8 servings

FRIED SHRIMP

1 cup of flour
½ teaspoon of sugar
1 egg, beaten
1 cup of ice water
2 tablespoons of oil
Salt and cayenne pepper, to taste
2 pounds of peeled and deveined shrimp
Oil for frying

1. Combine all ingredients except shrimp and oil for frying and beat well; place in refrigerator for 30 minutes.
2. Dry shrimp thoroughly on paper towels and dip into batter.
3. Fry in hot oil at 375 degrees until golden brown; drain on paper towels.

Yield: 4 to 6 servings

SHRIMP AND RICE

1 cup of chopped onions
½ cup of chopped celery
½ cup of chopped bell pepper
4 cloves of garlic, minced
½ cup of butter
2 tablespoons of tomato paste
2 cups of water
Salt, black pepper and cayenne pepper, to taste
1 teaspoon of sugar
2 pounds of peeled and deveined shrimp, chopped
½ teaspoon of cornstarch
2 cups of cooked rice
½ cup of chopped green onions
½ cup of chopped parsley

1. Saute onion, celery, bell pepper and garlic in butter until onions are transparent; add tomato paste and cook, stirring constantly, for 15 minutes.
2. Add 1½ cups of the water, salt, black pepper, cayenne pepper and sugar and simmer for 40 minutes, stirring occasionally.
3. Add shrimp and continue cooking for about 15 minutes.
4. Dissolve cornstarch in remaining ½ cup of water and add to shrimp mixture; cook for about 5 minutes; mix ingredients with cooked rice and add green onions and parsley.

Yield: 6 servings

SHRIMP AND CRAB ETOUFFEE

4 large onions, chopped
2 bell peppers, chopped
4 stalks of celery, chopped
6 cloves of garlic, minced
½ cup of oil
3 pounds of shrimp, peeled and deveined
2 dozen fresh crabs, cleaned but leave meat
   in shell and claws (or use 2 pounds of crab meat)
½ cup of water
Salt and cayenne pepper, to taste
¼ cup of chopped parsley
¼ cup of chopped green onion tops

1. Saute onions, bell peppers, celery and garlic in oil until onions are transparent; add shrimp and cook on medium heat until shrimp are pink, about 10 minutes.
2. Add crabs in shell and claws (or fresh crab meat) and mix well; add water, cover and simmer about 30 minutes.
3. Add salt, cayenne pepper, parsley and green onion tops; serve over cooked rice.

Yield: 8 servings

SHRIMP IN TOMATO GRAVY

2 large onions, chopped
4 cloves of garlic, minced
1 stalk of celery, chopped
¼ bell pepper, chopped
¼ cup of oil
1 8-ounce can of tomato sauce
1 6-ounce can of tomato paste
1 cup of water
Salt, black pepper and cayenne pepper, to taste
1 pound of peeled shrimp, deveined

1. Saute onions, garlic, celery and bell pepper in oil until vegetables are transparent; add tomato sauce, tomato paste, water, salt, black pepper and cayenne pepper and simmer for about 1 hour.
2. Add shrimp and continue simmering for about 30 minutes.
3. Serve over cooked rice.

Yield: 4 servings

FRIED OYSTERS

1 egg, beaten
3 tablespoons of baking powder
Cayenne pepper, to taste
2 pints of fresh oysters, drained
1½ cups of flour
¼ cup of chopped parsley
Oil for frying

1. Combine egg, baking powder and cayenne pepper and mix well; soak oysters in this mixture.
2. Combine flour, parsley and cayenne pepper; dip oysters in this mixture and shake off excess flour.
3. Fry in deep, hot oil at 375 degrees until golden brown; drain on paper towels.

Yield: 4 to 6 servings

BAKED STUFFED OYSTERS

1 large onion, grated
2 cloves of garlic, minced
¼ cup of finely chopped celery
1 tablespoon of shortening
6 dozen oysters, coarsley chopped (reserve the liquid)
6 slices of toasted white bread
2 sprigs of parsley, finely chopped
½ cup of butter or oleo
Salt, black pepper, and cayenne pepper to taste
1 egg, beaten
Bread crumbs

1. Saute onion, garlic and celery in melted shortening until vegetables are transparent; add oysters and cook for about one minute.
2. Soak toasted bread in oyster liquid and squeeze dry; add to oyster mixture and mix well. (If mixture appears dry, add some of the oyster liquid.)
3. Add parsley, six tablespoons of butter, salt, black pepper, cayenne pepper and egg and mix well.
4. Place mixture in buttered oyster shells or ramekins, sprinkle with bread crumbs and dot with remaining two tablespoons of butter; bake 20 minutes at 400 degrees.

Yield: 8 servings

Note: May be baked in a casserole dish; bake for 30 minutes.

CAJUN STUFFED OYSTERS

**1 pound of fresh pork sausage, removed from casing (See
   page 96)**
1 pint of oysters and oyster liquid, chopped
½ cup of chopped parsley
½ cup of chopped green onion tops
Crumbs from 8 slices of toasted bread
¼ cup of butter, melted
Juice of ½ lemon
12 oyster shells, cleaned and boiled for 5 minutes

1. Brown sausage slowly in a heavy pot; add oysters, parsley and
green onion tops and cook on medium heat for 10 minutes.
2. Add bread crumbs (you may not need all of them), butter and
lemon juice and mix well. If not moist enough, add some of the
oyster liquid.
3. Add salt and pepper if necessary and stuff mixture into the
oyster shells; place in a shallow pan and bake at 350 degrees for
25 minutes.

Yield: 12 stuffed oysters

Note: This can also be baked in individual ramekins or in a casserole
dish if oyster shells are not available.
If the sausage is highly seasoned, it might not be necessary to
add any salt and pepper.

SEAFOOD BOULETTES
IN TOMATO GRAVY

1 large onion, chopped
1 bell pepper, chopped
6 cloves of garlic, minced
½ cup of butter
2 10-ounce cans of tomatoes with chilies
2 16-ounce cans of tomato sauce
1 cup of chopped celery
Salt, black pepper and cayenne pepper, to taste
Seafood Boulettes (Recipe follows)

1. Saute onions, bell pepper and garlic in butter until onions are transparent; add tomatoes with chilies and tomato sauce and simmer for one hour.
2. Add celery, salt, black pepper and cayenne pepper and continue to cook for another hour.
3. Drop Seafood Boulettes in sauce and simmer about 30 minutes.

Seafood Boulettes

1 pound of peeled and deveined shrimp, ground
1 pound of peeled crawfish tails, ground
1 onion, grated
1 bell pepper, chopped fine
Salt and cayenne pepper, to taste

1. Mix all ingredients well.
2. Shape into balls about the size of a quarter.

SEAFOOD-STUFFED BELL PEPPERS

1 pound of peeled crawfish tails
1 pound of shrimp, peeled and deveined
½ cup of oil
1 large bell pepper, ground
½ cup of chopped onion
½ cup of chopped celery
1 teaspoon of cayenne pepper
Salt and black pepper, to taste
2 eggs
1 cup of bread crumbs, or 3 or 4 slices of bread
6 to 7 bell peppers, halved

1. Grind crawfish and shrimp and cook in oil until it turns pinkish-orange in color.
2. Add ground bell pepper, onion and celery and cook another 20 minutes, adding small amounts of water as needed to prevent sticking.
3. Add seasonings, let cool, then add eggs and stir well; add bread crumbs or stale bread and mix well.
4. Stuff into uncooked pepper shells.
5. Bake at 350 degrees for 20 to 30 minutes.

Yield: 12 to 14 servings

SEAFOOD STUFFED EGGPLANT

6 eggplants
2 onions, chopped
½ cup of butter
2 pounds of shrimp, peeled and deveined
1 pound of fresh crab meat
Salt, black pepper and cayenne pepper, to taste
8 slices of bread, soaked in ½ cup of milk
Bread crumbs

1. Boil eggplant in water to cover until slightly tender, about 20 to 30 minutes; cut each eggplant in half and scoop out the pulp, leaving about a ¼-inch shell. Reserve the eggplant pulp.
2. Saute onion in butter until onions are transparent; add eggplant pulp, shrimp, crab meat, salt, black pepper and cayenne pepper and continue to cook on medium heat for 10 to 15 minutes or until shrimp are pink.
3. Add sliced bread, gently squeezed dry, mix well and stuff into eggplant shells.
4. Dot with butter and sprinkle with bread crumbs; bake at 350 degrees for about 20 minutes or until brown.

Yield: 12 servings

SEAFOOD COCKTAIL SAUCE

⅔ cup of catsup
3 tablespoons of chili sauce
2 tablespoons of horseradish
3 tablespoons of fresh lemon juice
Hot pepper sauce, to taste

1. Mix all ingredients well; refrigerate until ready to serve.
2. This is served with any fried or boiled seafood.

Note: Minced onion may be added.

TARTAR SAUCE

1 cup of mayonnaise
2 tablespoons of dill pickle relish
1 small onion, grated
1 tablespoon of horseradish
Salt and hot pepper sauce, to taste

Combine all ingredients; let stand at least 30 minutes before serving. Serve with fried seafood.

Wild Game

WILD GAME

"These industrious Acadians, with survival uppermost in their minds, took the wild birds from the air, the fish from the bayous and the Gulf, the grain, vegetables and fruit from the land, and accepted customs from the Indians, Spaniards and Africans, then concocted and handed down recipes that are enjoyed by most of us here and sometimes by others who have the good fortune to taste our cuisine. Acadian recipes are in great demand."

BAKED DUCKS

6 wild ducks
Monosodium glutamate
½ cup of lemon juice (approximately)
¼ cup of salt (approximately)
Water
Cloves of garlic
Salt and pepper, to taste
8 to 12 strips of bacon
3 onions, cut into chunks
3 apples, chopped
3 stalks of celery, sliced
1 bell pepper, cut into chunks
¾ cup of butter or oleo
Flour or cornstarch

1. Sprinkle ducks with monosodium glutamate; place in large container with lemon juice, salt and enough water to cover. Marinate for at least three hours in refrigerator.
2. Wash ducks thoroughly in cold water; pat dry; stuff breasts with garlic.
3. Salt and pepper ducks (both outside and inside cavity); wrap each duck with two to three strips of bacon (depending on size of duck), securing bacon with toothpicks.
4. Combine onions, apples, celery, bell pepper and oleo; divide between the six ducks; stuff into cavities.
5. Bake at 425 degrees for about 30 minutes in covered roaster sprayed with spray coating and enough water to cover bottom of pan.
6. Turn oven down to 350 degrees; bake until tender, about two hours, basting occasionally; add water as needed.
7. Remove small or more tender ducks when tender; continue cooking others until done. If ducks are not brown enough (they usually are), remove cover and brown.
8. To make gravy, remove excess oil; thicken with flour and water if desired.

Yield: 8 to 10 servings

POT ROASTED DUCK OR GOOSE

2 wild ducks or 1 wild goose
Salt and cayenne pepper, to taste
1 onion, sliced
½ bell pepper, sliced
Slices of bacon
½ cup of oil

1. Season ducks or goose with salt and cayenne pepper; make a one-inch cut on each side of the breast, inserting the knife well into the breast.
2. Season onion slices with salt and cayenne pepper and put into cuts in the breast; put pieces of bell pepper into the cavity of the ducks or goose and lay slices of bacon over the top.
3. Heat oil in a heavy pot, add ducks or goose and cook, covered, on a low heat until ducks or goose are tender, about 2 hours or longer adding water, ½ cup at a time, as it cooks down.
4. Remove ducks or goose from pot, add enough water to drippings in pan to make a gravy and cook until gravy thickens.

Yield: 4 servings

DUCK SALAD

1 duck, boiled until tender and deboned
8 eggs, hard-boiled and mashed
6 to 8 sweet midget pickles, chopped
3 stalks of celery, chopped
1 bell pepper, chopped
Mayonnaise

1. Mix first five ingredients together in a large bowl.
2. Add mayonnaise; mix well.

Yield: 6 to 8 servings

WILD DUCK FRICASSEE WITH TURNIPS

1 tablespoon of oil
1 tablespoon of flour
1 large onion, chopped
1 stalk of celery, chopped
1 large wild duck, cut into serving pieces
1 large turnip, peeled and diced
¼ cup of chopped green onions
Salt, black pepper and cayenne pepper, to taste
2 tablespoons of chopped parsley

1. Make a dark brown roux with oil and flour; add onion, celery and cook until onions are transparent.
2. Add duck, turnips and green onions; smother for 10 minutes, stirring often.
3. Add enough water to barely cover ducks; add salt, black pepper and cayenne pepper and cook on medium-low heat until duck is tender, about 1½ hours. (You may have to add small amounts of water before the ducks are done.)
4. Add parsley and serve over cooked rice.

Yield: 4 servings

QUAIL WITH LEMON BUTTER

½ **cup of oleo**
¼ **cup of lemon juice**
8 quail
Salt and cayenne pepper, to taste
Bacon

1. Melt oleo and add lemon juice; brush inside and outside of quail with this mixture.
2. Season with salt and pepper and wrap each quail with strips of bacon.
3. Place in a baking pan, cover with foil and bake for about one hour, basting with remaining lemon-butter sauce; uncover and continue baking for 15 minutes or until brown.

Yield: 4 servings

SMOTHERED QUAIL OR DOVES

8 quail, cleaned
Salt, black pepper and cayenne pepper, to taste
½ **cup of oil**
2 onions, chopped
½ **bell pepper, chopped**
4 stalks of celery, chopped
½ **cup of water**

1. Season quail with salt, black pepper and cayenne pepper; brown in oil.
2. Add onions, bell pepper and celery and cook until onions are transparent.
3. Add water and simmer quail on low heat until tender, about 45 minutes.

Yield: 4 servings

STUFFED DOVE

12 doves, cleaned
Salt and pepper, to taste
Cloves of garlic
4 onions (2 cups chopped and the rest in wedges)
2 bell peppers, cut in chunks
¼ cup of oil
2 cups or more of water

1. Season doves well with salt and pepper.
2. Slit each side of breast; insert garlic clove in each slit.
3. Fill cavities with wedges of onions and bell peppers.
4. Pour oil into heavy iron pot and heat; add birds; cook until well-browned.
5. Add two cups of chopped onions; cook until wilted.
6. Add water; cook over medium heat, about 40 minutes, until tender. (If more water is needed, add gradually.)

Yield: 6 servings

ROASTED STUFFED SQUAB

2 cups of uncooked rice
4 cups of chicken stock
6 slices of bacon
¾ cup of chopped celery
1 onion, chopped
4 eggs, beaten
Salt, black pepper and cayenne pepper, to taste
4 squabs, cleaned
Sweet pickle juice

1. Cook rice in chicken stock according to instructions for cooking rice.
2. Dice bacon and fry until crisp; remove bacon and saute celery and onions in bacon drippings.
3. Add bacon, onions and celery to cooked rice, mixing well.
4. Add eggs, salt, black pepper and cayenne pepper and mix well; stuff squab cavity with some of the rice mixture.
5. Place remaining rice mixture in a baking dish and put stuffed squabs on top of rice; bake 25 minutes at 400 degrees, basting frequently with sweet pickle juice.

Yield: 4 servings

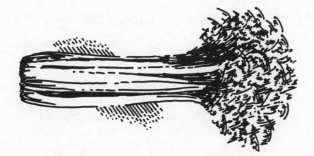

LAPIN AU SAUCE PIQUANTE
Rabbit Sauce Piquante

1 large rabbit, cut into serving pieces
Salt, black pepper and cayenne pepper, to taste
½ cup of oil
3 cups of chopped onion
1 large bell pepper, chopped
½ stalk of celery, chopped
2 teaspoons of garlic powder
2 fresh cayenne peppers, chopped
   (or ground cayenne pepper, to taste)
2 10-ounce cans of tomatoes with chilies
1 cup of chopped green onion tops
½ cup of chopped parsley

1. Season rabbit with salt, black pepper and cayenne pepper and brown in oil in a large heavy pot; when pieces are brown remove from pot.
2. Add onion, bell pepper and celery to the same pot and cook until onions are transparent; add garlic powder, fresh cayenne pepper and tomatoes and cook slowly until grease begins to rise to the top.
3. Add rabbit, cover with hot water and cook slowly for about two hours or until rabbit is tender. More water may be needed during the two hours.
5. Add green onion tops and parsley and cook 10 minutes; serve with cooked rice.

Yield: 4 to 6 servings

SQUIRREL GUMBO

7 tablespoons of flour
3 tablespoons of oil
3 quarts of water
4 to 5 small squirrels, cut into serving pieces
1 large onion, chopped
Salt and cayenne pepper, to taste
1 pound of smoked sausage, cut into bite-size pieces
¼ cup of chopped green onion tops
¼ cup of chopped parsley

1. Make a dark brown roux with flour and oil in a large heavy pot; add water and cook on high heat until roux dissolves and water is simmering.
2. Add squirrels, onions, salt and cayenne pepper and cook on medium heat for 30 minutes; add sausage and continue to cook for 1 to 1½ hours.
3. Add green onion tops and parsley; serve in soup bowls over cooked rice.

Yield: 12 servings

ALLIGATOR STEW

2 pounds of alligator meat, cut into small pieces about ½ inch thick
½ cup of oil
½ cup of chopped green onions
½ cup of chopped onion
½ cup of chopped bell pepper
½ cup of chopped celery
2 tablespoons of minced parsley
1 10-ounce can of tomatoes with chilies
Salt and pepper, to taste

1. Brown meat in oil; add remaining ingredients. Cover pot; cook over medium heat for 30 to 40 minutes.
2. Serve over cooked rice.

Yield: 6 to 8 servings

BUTTERED FROG LEGS

2 onions, chopped
3 cloves of garlic, minced
1 lemon, sliced
Juice of one lemon
1 tablespoon of salt
Cayenne pepper, to taste
8 frog legs
1½ cups of butter

1. Combine onion, garlic, lemon slices, lemon juice, salt and pepper.
2. Marinate frog legs in lemon mixture for about one hour, turning legs often.
3. Drain frog legs and saute in butter over medium-low heat until frog legs are lightly brown, about 10 minutes.

Yield: 4 servings

FRIED FROG LEGS

8 frog legs
Salt, black pepper and cayenne pepper, to taste
2 eggs, beaten
½ cup of milk
1 cup of flour
Oil for frying

1. Season frog legs with salt, black pepper and cayenne pepper; combine eggs and milk.
2. Dip frog legs into egg mixture and then into flour; fry in oil at 375 degrees until golden brown, about 6 to 8 minutes.

Yield: 4 servings

VENISON SUPREME

6 to 8 small venison steaks or chops
Salt, black pepper and cayenne pepper, to taste
½ cup of oil
1½ pounds of fresh pork sausage, removed from casing (See page 96)
3 large onions, chopped
1 large bell pepper, chopped
4 stalks of celery, chopped
2 teaspoons of garlic powder
1½ cups of water
½ cup of chopped parsley
½ cup of chopped green onion tops
1 red apple, peeled and chopped

1. Season venison with salt, black pepper and cayenne pepper; brown in a heavy pot in hot oil.
2. Remove venison from pot when brown; add pork sausage and brown; add onions, bell pepper, celery and garlic powder and cook until onions are transparent.
3. Return venison to pot and add water; simmer until venison is tender, about 1½ hours.
4. Add parsley, green onion tops and apple; continue cooking for 10 minutes.

Yield: 4 servings

VENISON ROAST

5 to 6 pounds of venison roast
Salt, black pepper and cayenne pepper to taste
3 tablespoons of minced garlic
2 large bell peppers, chopped
3 large onions, chopped
1 cup of white wine
2 6-ounce cans of apple juice

1. Season venison with salt, black pepper, cayenne pepper and garlic; place in a roasting pan and add bell pepper and onion.
2. Pour wine and apple juice over roast; cover and refrigerate for at least 24 hours.
3. Bake, covered, at 325 degrees for about 2 hours, basting often.

Yield: 8 servings

Jambalayas
Dressings
Casseroles

JAMBALAYAS, DRESSINGS AND CASSEROLES

"ACADIAN JAMBALAYA is not a mixture of boiled rice and gravy made from giblets, herbs and seasonings. Boiled rice and gravy is rice dressing. Jambalaya is the completed product of the skillful blending of many flavors of which none predominates."

CABBAGE CASSEROLE

1 pound of lean ground pork
2 tablespoons of oil
4 large onions, sliced
1 16-ounce can of tomato sauce
1 10-ounce can of tomatoes with green chilies
2 large heads of cabbage, cut in chunks
½ pound of sharp cheddar cheese, grated
Salt, black pepper and cayenne pepper, to taste

1. Brown pork in oil in a large pot; add onion, tomato sauce and tomatoes and simmer about 10 minutes.
2. Add cabbage and cook on low heat until cabbage is tender, about 20 minutes.
3. Place in baking dish and top with cheese; bake at 350 degrees for about 15 minutes or until cheese is melted.

Yield: 8 to 10 servings

POTATO HASH

1 large onion, chopped
3 tablespoons of oil
6 medium potatoes, peeled and cubed
1½ cups of water
1½ to 2 cups of cooked, leftover meat
Salt, black pepper and cayenne pepper, to taste
2 tablespoons of chopped parsley

1. Saute onion in oil until onions are transparent; add potatoes, stirring well to mix with onions, and cook about 3 to 4 minutes.
2. Add water, meat, salt, black pepper and cayenne pepper and cook covered over medium heat until potatoes are tender, about 20 minutes.
3. Add parsley and serve.

Yield: 4 to 6 servings

SEAFOOD AND EGGPLANT CASSEROLE

½ cup of chopped onions
½ cup of chopped celery
¼ cup of butter
2 eggplants, peeled, diced, boiled and drained
1 cup of bread crumbs
1 pound of boiled shrimp, peeled and chopped
½ pound of crab meat
2 eggs, beaten
¼ cup of chopped green onion tops
¼ cup of chopped parsley
Salt, black pepper and cayenne pepper, to taste

1. Saute onions and celery in butter until onions are transparent; add eggplant and simmer 15 minutes.
2. Add bread crumbs, shrimp and crab meat and gently mix; add eggs, green onion tops, parsley, salt, black pepper and cayenne pepper and mix.
3. Place in a casserole dish, top with additional bread crumbs and bake at 400 degrees for 30 minutes or until browned.

Yield: 6 servings

MIRLITON CASSEROLE

4 mirlitons
1 large onion, chopped
½ small bell pepper, chopped
2 cloves of garlic, minced
½ cup of butter
1 pound of peeled and deveined shrimp
1 tablespoon of chopped parsley
Salt and cayenne pepper, to taste
2 cups of bread crumbs

1. Boil mirlitons about 45 minutes; peel, remove seed and chop into small pieces.
2. Saute onion, bell pepper and garlic in butter until onions are transparent; add shrimp, mirlitons, parsley, salt and cayenne pepper.
3. Cook over medium heat, stirring often for about 20 minutes; remove from heat, add one cup of the bread crumbs and mix well.
4. Place in a greased casserole dish, top with remaining cup of bread crumbs and bake at 350 degrees for 30 minutes.

Yield: 6 to 8 servings

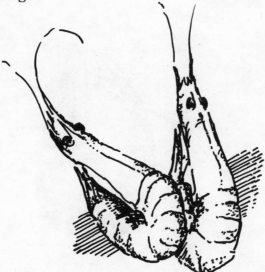

EGGPLANT CASSEROLE

2 eggplants, peeled and diced
½ cup of water
¼ teaspoon of oregano
¼ teaspoon of salt
Cayenne pepper, to taste
1 pound of ground veal or beef
1 onion, chopped
1 clove of garlic, minced
Bread crumbs from 3 slices of bread
1 egg, beaten
⅛ teaspoon of cinnamon
½ cup of canned tomato sauce
Grated cheddar cheese

1. Simmer eggplant, water, oregano, salt, and cayenne pepper in a covered saucepan for 15 minutes; drain water and mash eggplant with a fork.
2. Brown veal or beef with onion and garlic until onions are transparent; drain excess grease.
3. Add bread crumbs, egg and cinnamon and mix well; place in a greased 1½-quart casserole dish and pour tomato sauce over the top.
4. Sprinkle with grated cheese and bake uncovered at 350 degrees for 30 to 40 minutes.

Yield: 4 to 6 servings

CAJUN MELANGE

1½ cups of cooked lamb, veal or chicken, diced
   (meat should be cold)
1 cup of cooked rice
1½ cups of cooked or canned tomatoes, chopped
1 onion, chopped
½ bell pepper, chopped
2 stalks of celery, chopped
1 teaspoon of salt
1 teaspoon of cayenne pepper
Buttered bread crumbs

1. Mix meat, rice and tomatoes in a heavy skillet and cook for 10 minutes.
2. Add onions, bell pepper and celery and cook 30 minutes; season with salt and cayenne pepper.
3. Place mixture in a buttered baking dish; cover with bread crumbs.
4. Bake one hour at 350 degrees.

Yield: 4 servings

CABBAGE DRESSING

1 pound of fresh pork sausage (See page 96)
½ cup of flour
½ cup of oil
1 small onion, chopped
2 cups of water
1 cabbage (1½ to 2 pounds), cut into large pieces
2 cups of cooked rice or more
Salt, black pepper and cayenne pepper, to taste

1. Brown sausage, remove from pan and cut into 1½ to 2-inch pieces.
2. Make a light brown roux with flour and oil; add onion and cook until onions are transparent.
3. Add water and bring to a boil; add cabbage and cook for 15 to 20 minutes.
4. Add sausage and cook until oil rises to the top, about 30 minutes; add cooked rice, salt, black pepper and cayenne pepper and mix well. More rice may be added if dressing is too moist.
5. Cover the pot and cook on a very low heat for about 10 minutes.
Yield: 4 to 6 servings

BLACK-EYED PEA DRESSING

1 pound of dried or fresh black-eyed peas
1 onion, chopped
1 clove of garlic, minced
1 quart of water
Salt, black pepper and cayenne pepper, to taste
½ pound of smoked ham, chopped (optional)
¼ cup of chopped parsley
½ cup of chopped green onion tops
2 cups of raw rice, cooked

1. Combine peas, onion, garlic, water, salt, black pepper, cayenne pepper and ham (if desired) in a heavy pot; bring to a boil, lower heat and cook until peas are tender and creamy (45 minutes for fresh peas and 2 hours for dried peas).
2. Add cooked rice, mixing gently until rice is coated with pea mixture; add parsley and green onion tops and mix.
Yield: 8 to 10 servings

CRAWFISH DRESSING

2 cups of finely chopped onions
1 clove of garlic, minced
1 cup of butter
2 pounds of crawfish tails with fat (if available)
Salt, black pepper and cayenne pepper, to taste
1 teaspoon of paprika
½ cup of chopped green onion tops
½ cup of chopped parsley
3 cups of cooked rice

1. Saute onions and garlic in butter until onions are transparent; add fat from crawfish (if available), stir well and simmer for 10 minutes. If crawfish fat is not available, omit this step.
2. Add crawfish tails, salt, black pepper, cayenne pepper and paprika and simmer for 15 minutes on low heat, stirring often.
3. Add cooked green onion tops, parsley and cooked rice, mixing gently.

Yield: 8 to 10 servings

EGGPLANT DRESSING

¾ **pound of ground beef**
¾ **pound of ground pork**
2 onions, chopped
3 stalks of celery, chopped
½ **bell pepper, chopped**
4 large eggplants, peeled and chopped
1 cup of water
Salt, black pepper, and cayenne pepper, to taste
3 cups of cooked rice

1. Brown ground beef and ground pork; add onion, celery, and bell pepper and cook until onions are transparent.
2. Add eggplant and water and simmer until eggplant is thoroughly mashed; add salt, black pepper and cayenne pepper and mix well.
3. Add rice, mix well and serve.

Yield: 8 servings

EGGPLANT RICE DRESSING

1 tablespoon of shortening
2 large eggplants, peeled and diced
½ **cup of chopped onion**
½ **cup of chopped bell pepper**
2 cups of chopped celery
3 cups of cooked rice
1 teaspoon of black pepper

1. Heat shortening for three minutes; add eggplant, onion, bell pepper and celery; stir and cook for about 30 minutes.
2. Remove mixture from pot and put it into a large mixing bowl; add rice and pepper and fluff rice with a fork.

Yield: 8 servings

GUINEA RICE DRESSING

1 guinea, cleaned and cut into serving pieces
2 medium chopped onions
3 stalks of celery, chopped
4 cups of water
¼ cup of oil
5 cups of cooked rice
½ cup of chopped parsley
Salt, black pepper and cayenne pepper, to taste

1. Brown guinea in oil; remove from pan, cool slightly and debone.
2. Add onions and celery to the pan of oil and cook until onions are transparent; add remaining ingredients except rice; cover and cook on low heat until guinea is tender, about 2 hours.
3. Add rice and mix well.

Yield: 6-8 servings

OYSTER AND RICE DRESSING

1 pint of chicken liver
1 pint of chicken gizzards
¼ cup of oil
1 onion, chopped
2 bell peppers, chopped
½ stalk of celery, chopped
6 cups of cooked rice
Salt, black pepper and cayenne pepper, to taste
1 pint of fresh oysters

1. Boil liver and gizzards in water to cover until tender, about 30 minutes; save broth and grind liver and gizzards in food processor or grinder.
2. In oil, saute onion, bell pepper and celery until onions are transparent; add ground liver and gizzards; simmer for 15 minutes; then add cooked rice and enough broth to make dressing moist.
3. Season dressing with salt, black pepper and cayenne pepper; add oysters and mix well.
4. Dressing may be used to stuff a turkey or hen, or it may be placed in a buttered casserole dish and baked at 325 degrees for 45 minutes.

Yield: 8 servings

OYSTER DRESSING

½ cup of butter
2 medium onions, chopped
½ cup of chopped celery
½ cup of chopped bell pepper
4 teaspoons of chopped parsley
½ cup of chopped green onions
Salt, black pepper and cayenne pepper, to taste
3 dozen fresh oysters, coarsely chopped
  (reserve the oyster liquid)
4 cups of cubed French bread

1. Melt butter in a heavy saucepan; saute remaining ingredients except oysters and bread until onions are transparent.
2. Add oysters and simmer about 15 minutes; add bread and mix well. (If mixture seems too thick, add some of the reserved oyster liquid.)

Yield: 6 to 8 servings

Note: Serve this as a side dish with roast beef, turkey, or wild game.

SAUSAGE DRESSING

1 pound of fresh pork sausage (See page 96)
1 cup of chopped onions
½ cup of chopped bell peppers
4 stalks of celery, chopped
1 10-ounce can of tomatoes with chilies
½ cup of tomato sauce
1 16-ounce can of whole kernel corn
2 cups of cooked long grain rice
1 bunch of green onion tops, chopped
½ cup of cooked parsley
Salt, black pepper and cayenne pepper, to taste

1. Brown sausage in a large, heavy pot; remove from pot and cut into 1½-inch pieces.
2. Add onions, bell pepper and celery to pot and cook until onions are transparent; add sausage, tomatoes and tomato sauce to vegetables and simmer for 30 minutes.
3. Add corn (including liquid) and continue cooking for another 15 minutes; add rice, green onion tops, parsley, salt, black pepper and cayenne pepper and mix well. It may not be necessary to add all of the rice; dressing should be moist.
4. Place in buttered casserole and bake at 350 degrees for about 20 minutes.

Yield: 4 to 6 servings

SQUASH DRESSING

½ cup of oil
12 to 15 yellow squash, sliced, or 18 ounces of frozen squash
1 bell pepper, chopped
1 onion, chopped
1 stalk of celery, chopped
1 teaspoon of garlic salt
½ teaspoon of salt
1 bay leaf
Dash of nutmeg
2 cups of cornbread crumbs
2 beaten eggs
½ cup of grated cheese

1. Mix the oil, squash, bell pepper, onion, celery, salts, bay leaf and nutmeg together and cook over low heat until vegetables are tender, about 30 minutes. Remove bay leaf.
2. Add the cornbread crumbs and eggs to the mixture.
3. Pour into a greased casserole and bake at 350 degrees for 20 minutes.
4. Sprinkle grated cheese over the top and return to oven for 10 minutes.

Yield: 8 servings

CAJUN RICE

½ cup of oil
½ cup of flour
1 pound of ground beef
1 pound of ground pork
½ pound of ground pork liver
1 bell pepper, chopped
3 onions, chopped
4 stalks of celery, chopped
1½ cups of water
Salt, black pepper and cayenne pepper, to taste
1 bunch of green onion tops, chopped
½ cup of minced parsley
3 cups of cooked rice

1. Make a light brown roux with oil and flour.
2. Saute beef, pork and liver in another pot until light brown; add bell pepper, onion and celery and continue cooking until onions are transparent.
3. Add roux and water to meat mixture and simmer 30 to 45 minutes.
4. Add salt, black pepper, cayenne pepper, green onion tops and parsley and mix well.
5. When ready to serve, add cooked rice and mix well.

Yield: 6 to 8 servings

RICE DRESSING

½ pound of ground pork
3 small onions, chopped fine
3 stalks of celery, chopped fine
1 large bell pepper, chopped fine
1½ pounds of chicken gizzards, boiled and ground
1 pound of chicken livers, boiled and ground
3 cups of broth from gizzards and livers
½ cup of dark brown roux
Salt, black pepper and cayenne pepper, to taste
½ cup of chopped green onions
½ cup of chopped parsley
2 cups of cooked rice

1. Brown pork in a large, heavy skillet; add onions, celery and bell pepper and cook until onions are transparent.
2. Add gizzards and livers and continue to cook for about 10 minutes; add broth, roux, salt, black pepper and cayenne pepper and continue to cook on medium heat for about one hour.
3. Add green onions, parsley and cooked rice and mix well. Add more cooked rice if dressing appears too moist.

Yield: 8 servings

SHRIMP JAMBALAYA

3 large onions, chopped
2 bell peppers, chopped
1 cup of oil
1 8-ounce can of tomato sauce
1 6-ounce can of tomato paste
½ cup of chopped green onion tops
½ cup of chopped parsley
2 cloves of garlic, minced
6 cups of water
5 teaspoons of salt
Black pepper and cayenne pepper, to taste
2 bay leaves
4 cups of raw rice
2 pounds of peeled and deveined shrimp

1. Saute onions and bell peppers in oil over low heat until onions are transparent; add tomato sauce and tomato paste and cook on low heat for one hour.
2. Add remaining ingredients, stir well and bring to a boil; pour into a greased baking dish, cover and bake at 300 degrees for one hour or until rice is cooked.

Yield: 8 servings

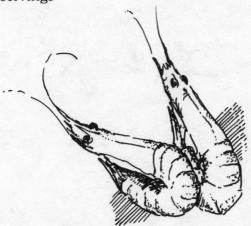

PORK RIB JAMBALAYA

4 pounds of pork ribs, cut in one-inch pieces
Salt, black pepper and cayenne pepper, to taste
1 tablespoon of oil
2 onions, chopped
1 bell pepper, chopped
3½ cups of water
1½ cups of rice
½ cup of chopped green onions
½ cup of chopped parsley

1. Season pork ribs with salt and peppers and brown in oil; remove excess grease and add onion, bell pepper and 2 cups of the water.
2. Boil until ribs are tender, about one hour; add remaining 1½ cups of water and rice, and mix well.
3. Cover and bring to a boil over high heat; lower heat, carefully scrape bottom of pot with a spatula to turn rice over and cook covered until rice is tender, about 20 minutes.
4. Correct seasoning; add green onions and parsley and serve.

Yield: 6 servings

SAUSAGE JAMBALAYA

2 pounds of smoked sausage
½ cup of oil
1 large onion, chopped
2 stalks of celery, chopped
1 medium bell pepper, chopped
2 cups of uncooked rice
4 cups of water
Salt, black pepper and cayenne, to taste
½ cup of chopped green onions
½ cup of chopped parsley

1. Cut smoked sausage into four-inch links and boil in two quarts of water for 25 minutes. Pour out excess water and slice sausage into bite-size pieces.
2. Brown sausage in heavy skillet in cooking oil until well-browned.
3. Add onion, celery and bell pepper and cook until onion is transparent.
4. Add rice and water, along with seasonings. Cover and cook over low heat, stirring frequently. (If rice does not seem to be cooking thoroughly through the process, continue adding water in small amounts until cooked and no longer mushy, perhaps one hour.)
5. Add green onions and parsley just before serving.

Yield: 6 to 8 servings

CHICKEN JAMBALAYA

1 hen, cut into serving pieces
Salt and cayenne pepper, to taste
½ cup of oil
3 onions, chopped
½ cup of canned tomatoes, chopped
1 cup of celery, chopped
2 quarts of water
1 teaspoon of basil
1 bay leaf
2 teaspoons of hot pepper sauce
3 cups of uncooked rice
½ cup of chopped green onions
½ cup of chopped parsley

1. Season hen with salt and cayenne pepper; brown in oil in a large heavy pot and remove from pot as pieces brown.
2. Add onions and saute until onions are transparent; add tomatoes, celery, hen, water, basil, bay leaf and more salt and cayenne pepper; bring water to a boil, lower heat and simmer until hen is tender, about 1½ to 2 hours. Add water during cooking to keep water at the same level.
3. Add rice, cover pot and cook on very low heat about one hour; add green onions and parsley and continue to cook until rice is tender.

Yield: 6 to 8 servings

CRAWFISH JAMBALAYA

2 onions, chopped
1 bell pepper, chopped
4 stalks of celery, chopped
6 tablespoons of bacon drippings
2 cups of uncooked rice
4 cups of water
2 pounds of crawfish tails, peeled
2 teaspoons of salt
1 teaspoon of pepper
½ teaspoon of garlic powder

1. Saute onions, bell pepper and celery in bacon drippings until onions are transparent.
2. Remove vegetables; add rice and cook until brown.
3. Return vegetables to browned rice; add water. Cover with a tight-fitting lid and simmer for about 20 minutes.
4. Stir in crawfish and seasonings. Cover and cook an additional 25 minutes; add water if needed.

Yield: 12 servings

BEEF AND CABBAGE JAMBALAYA

1 head of cabbage, shredded
1 pound of ground meat
1 large onion, chopped
1 cup of raw rice
1 cup of water
Salt and pepper, to taste

1. Smother the cabbage, ground meat and onion.
2. Add rice, water and seasonings; cook on low heat for one hour.

Desserts

DESSERTS

GATEAU SIROP
Syrup Cake

½ cup of shortening
½ cup of sugar
1 cup of sugar cane syrup
2 eggs
2½ cups of sifted all-purpose flour
1 teaspoon of salt
2 teaspoons of baking soda
1 teaspoon of ginger
1 teaspoon of cinnamon
1 cup of hot water

1. Cream shortening and sugar until light and fluffy; mix in syrup.
2. Add eggs one at a time, beating well after each addition.
3. Sift together the flour, salt, baking soda, ginger and cinnamon; add to creamed mixture alternately with hot water.
4. Pour into a greased and floured 9-inch square pan and bake at 350 degrees for 40 minutes.

Yield: 8 servings

FIG CAKE

2 cups of sugar
1 cup of shortening
3 eggs, beaten well
2 cups of flour
1 teaspoon of cinnamon
1 teaspoon of cloves
1 teaspoon of nutmeg
½ teaspoon of baking soda
½ teaspoon of salt
1 cup of sour milk (add 2 tablespoons
   of vinegar to 1 cup of milk)
1 cup of chopped pecans
1 cup of mashed fig preserves

1. Cream sugar and shortening together until mixture is light and fluffy; add eggs, one at a time, beating after each addition.
2. Combine flour, cinnamon, cloves, nutmeg, baking soda and salt; add to egg mixture, alternating with sour milk, and mix well.
3. Stir in pecans and fig preserves. This recipe makes enough batter for one tube cake and one loaf cake.
4. Grease and flour a tube cake pan and a loaf pan; pour in batter, filling pans half full, and bake at 300 degrees for 1 to 1½ hours, until a toothpick comes out clean.

LOUISIANA PEAR CAKE

½ cup of oleo, softened
1 cup of sugar
1 egg
1½ cups of flour
¼ teaspoon of salt
1 teaspoon of baking soda
½ teaspoon of cinnamon
1 teaspoon of vanilla
2 cups of grated raw pears
½ cup of chopped pecans

1. Mix oleo, sugar and egg together.
2. Sift flour, salt, soda and cinnamon together; add to sugar and egg mixture.
3. Add vanilla, pears and nuts and mix well.
4. Pour into a greased and floured baking dish or pan 8x8x2 inches.
5. Bake at 300 degrees for one hour; serve with whipped cream.

POUND CAKE

½ pound of butter
2 cups of sugar
4 eggs
3 cups of cake flour
2 teaspoons of baking powder
1 cup of milk
2 teaspoons of lemon juice
Glaze (Recipe follows)

1. Cream butter and sugar together; add eggs, one at a time, beating after each addition.
2. Sift flour and baking powder together; add alternately with milk to egg mixture.
3. Add lemon juice and beat for 3 minutes; pour into a well-greased and floured tube pan and bake at 325 degrees for one hour.
4. Pour Glaze over hot cake and return to oven for 3 minutes. Do not remove from the pan until cake is cool.

Glaze

1½ cups of powdered sugar
2 tablespoons of orange juice
2 tablespoons of lemon juice

Mix all ingredients together.

LE GATEAU AU VIN
Wine Cake

½ **pound of butter**
2 **cups of sugar**
1 **teaspoon of vanilla**
5 **tablespoons of cocoa**
4 **eggs, separated**
2 **cups of chopped pecans**
2 **cups of raisins**
½ **apple, peeled and finely chopped**
4 **cups of flour**
1 **teaspoon of baking soda**
1 **cup of semi-sweet red wine**

1. Cream butter and sugar together until light and fluffy; add vanilla and cocoa and beat until well blended.
2. Add egg yolks to creamed mixture and beat well.
3. Place pecans, raisins and apple in a paper bag with one cup of the flour and shake well to coat the ingredients.
4. Mix baking soda with the wine; add wine mixture alternately with the remaining three cups of flour to the creamed mixture and mix well.
5. Add the pecans, raisins and apple to the batter and mix well.
6. Beat egg whites until they form soft peaks; fold into the batter.
7. Place in a buttered tube pan and bake at 300 degrees for about 1½ hours.

HOT MILK CAKE

3 eggs at room temperature
1 cup of sugar
¾ cup of flour
1 teaspoon of baking powder
¼ teaspoon of salt
½ cup of scalded milk
1 teaspoon of vanilla
Topping (Recipe follows)

1. Beat eggs until thick; gradually beat in sugar.
2. Combine flour, baking powder and salt; add to egg mixture and mix well.
3. Stir in milk and vanilla; pour into an ungreased 10-inch black iron skillet or 9-inch square cake pan and bake 30 minutes at 350 degrees.
4. Spread Topping over warm cake and broil 6 inches from heat until topping bubbles and browns slightly; serve cake warm.

Topping

⅓ cup of brown sugar
2 tablespoons of butter
½ cup of chopped pecans
1 cup of grated coconut
2 tablespoons of milk

1. Cream brown sugar and butter together.
2. Add pecans and coconut and mix well; stir in milk.

CAJUN GINGER CAKE

1 cup of sugar
1 cup of oil
1 cup of sugar cane syrup
3 tablespoons of black molasses
2 cups plus 2 tablespoons of flour
½ teaspoon of baking powder
3 eggs
1 teaspoon of baking soda
¾ cup of hot water
1 teaspoon of ginger
1 teaspoon of cinnamon

1. Beat sugar, oil, sugar cane syrup and molasses together; combine flour and baking powder.
2. Add flour to syrup mixture alternately with the eggs, stirring well after each addition.
3. Mix baking soda and hot water; add with ginger and cinnamon to batter and mix well.
4. Pour into a 9 × 14 inch greased baking pan and bake at 350 degrees for 35 to 40 minutes.

TARTE A LA BOUILLIE
Custard Pie

⅔ cup of sugar
6 tablespoons of flour
¼ teaspoon of salt
2 eggs, beaten
2 cups of milk
2 teaspoons of vanilla
Sweet Crust (Recipe follows)

1. Mix sugar, flour and salt, add eggs and beat well.
2. Bring milk to a boil; add egg mixture and cook over medium heat untl thick.
3. Cool and add vanilla; pour into unbaked sweet crust pie shell and top with a lattice top crust.
4. Bake at 350 degrees for 30 to 35 minutes or until golden brown; serve warm.

Sweet Crust

¾ cup of shortening
1½ cups of sugar
½ cup of milk (mixed with 1 tablespoon of vinegar)
1 egg, beaten
3½ cups of flour
1 teaspoon of baking soda
½ teaspoon of salt
Grated nutmeg

1. Cream shortening and sugar; add milk and egg and mix well.
2. Sift remaining ingredients and add to milk mixture, mixing well.
3. Chill at least two hours before rolling crust; roll and fit into a nine-inch pie plate.
4. Roll remaining dough and cut for a lattice top.

Yield: 8 servings

PECAN PIE

3 tablespoons of butter
¾ cup of sugar
3 eggs
⅛ teaspoon of salt
¾ cup of white corn syrup
¼ cup of honey
1 teaspoon of vanilla
1½ cups of chopped pecans
1 unbaked pastry shell
½ cup of pecan halves (optional)

1. Cream butter and sugar together; add eggs and salt and beat well.
2. Add syrup and honey; beat and add vanilla, mixing well.
3. Place chopped pecans in the bottom of the pastry shell, pour filling over chopped pecans and place pecan halves on top (if desired).
4. Bake at 350 degrees for 50 to 55 minutes.

Yield: 8 servings

MOLASSES PECAN PIE

1 cup of sugar
½ cup of molasses
1 tablespoon of vinegar
¼ cup of butter
3 eggs, well beaten
1 cup of chopped pecans
¼ teaspoon of allspice
¼ teaspoon of nutmeg
1 unbaked pastry shell

1. Mix sugar, molasses, vinegar and butter in a saucepan and bring to a boil; cook one minute and cool slightly.
2. Stir mixture into eggs, beating well; add pecans, allspice and nutmeg and mix.
3. Pour into pastry shell and bake at 350 degrees for 50 to 60 minutes or until mixture is set.

Yield: 8 servings

BLACKBERRY PIE

2 quarts of fresh blackberries
3 cups of sugar
1 tablespoon of flour
Double-crust pastry shell
2 tablespoons of butter

1. Mix blackberries with sugar and let mixture set about one hour; cook on medium-low heat until mixture is clear or until it reaches 220 degrees on a candy thermometer.
2. Sprinkle flour on the bottom of the pie crust; pour in blackberry filling and dot with butter.
3. Top with a lattice crust; bake at 375 degrees about 25 minutes or until crust is golden brown.

LEMON PIE

1 cup plus 2 tablespoons of sugar
3 tablespoons of cornstarch
Juice of 2 lemons
2 teaspoons of grated lemon rind
3 egg yolks
1¼ cups of hot tap water
3 egg whites
Baked pastry shell

1. Mix one cup of the sugar, cornstarch, lemon juice and lemon rind in a heavy saucepan.
2. Beat egg yolks and add to lemon mixture in saucepan; add hot water and cook over medium heat until thick.
3. Pour into baked pie shell.
4. Beat egg whites until stiff with two tablespoons of the sugar; spread over lemon filling.
5. Bake at 350 degrees for 15 minutes or until brown.

BLACKBERRY COBBLER

2 quarts of fresh blackberries
3 cups of sugar
1 tablespoon of flour
2 tablespoons of butter
Biscuit dough (See page 32)

1. Mix blackberries with sugar and let mixture set about one hour; cook on medium-low heat until mixture is clear or until it reaches 220 degrees on a candy thermometer. Cool.
2. Mix some of the blackberry juice with the flour and then add the flour mixture to the blackberries and mix well.
3. Roll biscuit dough out to about ¼-inch thickness; cut into strips.
4. Lay ¼ of the strips in the bottom of a 2-inch deep baking dish; add ⅓ of the blackberries and ⅓ of the butter.
5. Repeat this procedure two more times and top with the remaining ¼ of the biscuit dough in a crisscross manner.
6. Bake at 375 degrees about 25 to 30 minutes or until dough is golden brown.

Yield: 8 servings

CAJUN TARTS

½ cup of shortening
1 cup of sugar
1 egg
3 cups of flour
1 tablespoon of baking powder
½ cup of milk
1 teaspoon of vanilla
2 cups of fig or blackberry preserves (See page 214)

1. Cream shortening and sugar together; add egg and mix well.
2. Sift flour and baking powder together; add to batter alternately with milk and vanilla.
3. Roll out on floured board to ⅛-inch thickness; cut into 5-inch circles.
4. Put a spoon of preserves on ½ of the circle, fold pastry in half and seal with a fork; place on a cookie sheet and bake at 350 degrees for 15 to 20 minutes.

Yield: 8-10 tarts

Note: Cooked sweet potatoes, peaches, strawberries or pineapple can also be used as a filling.

OREILLES DE COCHON
Pastries shaped like pigs ears

1 egg
½ cup of milk
2 cups of flour
2 teaspoons of baking powder
½ teaspoon of salt
Oil for frying
1 cup of sugar cane syrup
1 cup of chopped pecans

1. Beat egg until foamy; add milk and blend.
2. Sift flour, baking powder and salt together twice; add to egg mixture and blend.
3. Cut off small portions of dough about the size of a walnut and roll on a lightly floured board until very thin.
4. Drop each piece into hot oil at 375 degrees and give each piece a twist from the top with a fork; fry until light brown and drain on paper towels.
5. Boil sugar cane syrup until it forms a soft ball in cold water and drizzle over the fried pastries.
6. While syrup is still hot, drop chopped pecans onto the pastries.

Yield: 4 to 5 dozen

STAGE PLANK

1 cup of sugar cane syrup
1 cup of butter
1 teaspoon of ginger
1 cup of sour milk (add 2 tablespoons
**   of vinegar to 1 cup of milk)**
1 teaspoon of baking soda
1 tablespoon of boiling water
3 cups of flour

1. Heat syrup, butter and ginger in a saucepan on a low heat; when butter is melted, remove from heat and add sour milk.
2. Beat this mixture for 10 minutes.
3. Mix baking soda in the boiling water and add to the syrup mixture, beating well.
4. Add flour, a little at a time, beating well.
5. Roll dough on a floured board to about ¼-inch thickness and cut into pieces about 2 inches wide and 3 inches long.
6. Place on a buttered cookie sheet and bake at 400 degrees for 10 minutes.

TEACAKES

1 cup plus 2 tablespoons of shortening
1¾ cups of sugar
4 eggs
5 cups of flour
Grated nutmeg, to taste
5 teaspoons of baking powder

1. Cream shortening and sugar; add eggs, one at a time, beating after each addition.
2. Sift 4½ cups of the flour, nutmeg and baking powder together and add to sugar mixture, mixing well.
3. Use about ½ cup of the flour on a board and roll dough to about ¼-inch thick; cut into 2-inch round shapes with a cookie cutter.
4. Bake on a cookie sheet at 375 degrees for 7 minutes on the middle shelf of the oven; move to a higher shelf and continue baking for 3 minutes.
Yield: 6 dozen teacakes

BANANA FRITTERS

1¼ cups of sifted flour
2 teaspoons of baking powder
1¼ teaspoons of salt
1 tablespoon of granulated sugar
1 egg, beaten
⅓ cup of milk
2 teaspoons of melted butter or shortening
2 to 3 firm bananas, peeled and cut into 3 or 4
    diagonal pieces
Oil for frying
Powdered sugar

1. Sift one cup of the flour, baking powder, salt and granulated sugar together.
2. Combine egg, milk and melted butter; add to dry ingredients and mix until batter is smooth. This makes a stiff batter; it makes a crisp fritter and will stay crisp about 15 to 20 minutes after frying.
3. Roll bananas in remaining ¼ cup of flour; dip into fritter batter, completely coating pieces with batter.
4. Fry in oil at 375 degrees until brown, turning fritters to brown evenly on all sides; drain on paper towels; sprinkle when hot with powdered sugar.

Yield: 6 servings

LES CHOU CREME
Cream Puffs

1 cup of water
½ teaspoon of salt
½ cup of butter
1 cup of flour
4 eggs

1. Place water, salt and butter in a saucepan and bring to a boil; add flour, all at once, and beat until the mixture leaves the side of the pan.
2. Remove from the heat and cool slightly; add eggs, one at a time, beating vigorously after each addition.
3. Place dough by teaspoonfuls on a greased cookie sheet and bake at 400 degrees for 30 minutes; lower heat to 350 degrees and bake another 10 minutes.
4. Remove from oven and cut the top partially off; remove the filaments from the inside.
5. Cream puffs may be filled with a custard cream (see Tarte à la Bouillie, page 195) or any creamed meat or seafood (such as Crab Meat Au Gratin, page 124).

Yield: Approximately 2 dozen

AMBROSIA

1 dozen oranges, peeled and sliced
1 fresh coconut, peeled and grated
1 cup of super-fine sugar
Maraschino cherries in juice, garnish

1. In a large, glass bowl make alternate layers of orange slices, grated coconut and a sprinkle of sugar; continue until all of the oranges and coconut have been used.
2. Garnish the top with cherries and drizzle cherry juice over top.

Yield: 8 servings

BREAD PUDDING

½ loaf of French bread
1 quart of milk
½ cup plus 8 teaspoons of sugar
4 whole eggs plus 4 egg whites
3 teaspoons of vanilla
1 cup of chopped pecans
1 cup of raisins
Pinch of cream of tartar

1. Break up the bread and soak in milk; add ½ cup of the sugar, 4 whole eggs, 2 teaspoons of the vanilla, pecans and raisins and mix well.
2. Bake in a greased 9 × 12 inch baking pan for 30 minutes at 350 degrees.
3. Beat egg whites with cream of tartar until stiff but not dry, gradually adding the 8 teaspoons of sugar; stir in the remaining 1 teaspoon of vanilla; spread meringue over bread pudding and bake 10 minutes or until brown.

COCOONS

½ cup of butter
3 tablespoons of sugar
1½ cups of sifted flour
1 teaspoon of vanilla
¾ cup of finely chopped pecans
Powdered sugar

1. Cream butter and sugar together; add flour, vanilla and nuts and mix well. Dough will be very stiff.
2. Shape into small balls or crescents and place on a greased cookie sheet; bake at 350 degrees for about 15 minutes. Cookies will not be brown.
3. Roll each cookie in powdered sugar.

SOUPIRS

4 egg whites
¼ teaspoon of cream of tartar
½ cup of sugar
Pinch of salt
½ teaspoon of vanilla or almond flavoring

1. Beat egg whites, cream of tartar and salt until the eggs hold soft peaks.
2. Continue beating, gradually adding sugar until stiff peaks are formed.
3. Add vanilla or almond flavoring and mix; drop by teaspoonfuls on a lightly greased cookie sheet and bake at 350 degrees about 15 to 20 minutes or until lightly brown.
4. Cool away from drafts.

COCONUT PRALINES

1 cup of coconut milk (from a fresh coconut)
2 cups of sugar
Pinch of salt
2 cups of grated fresh coconut
1 tablespoon of butter
1 teaspoon of vanilla

1. Combine coconut milk, sugar and salt and cook until the sugar is melted.
2. Add grated coconut and continue to cook while stirring until the syrup on the side of the pot begins to form crystals; remove from heat and add butter and vanilla.
3. Beat until the mixture begins to "pop" when stirring; place by teaspoonfuls on a cookie sheet and cool before serving.

PRALINES

2 cups of light brown sugar
½ cup of evaporated milk
¼ cup of butter
2⅓ cups of pecans (whole or chopped)
1 teaspoon of vanilla

1. Combine sugar and milk in a saucepan, bring to a boil and continue to cook until a drop forms a soft ball in cold water, stirring often.
2. Add butter and pecans; bring back to soft-ball stage while stirring.
3. Remove from heat, add vanilla and beat until mixture begins to thicken.
4. Drop by teaspoons on wax paper.

Yield: about 30 pieces

PECAN GLACE

1 cup of sugar
¼ teaspoon of cream of tartar
½ cup of water
2 cups of pecan halves

1. In a medium-size, heavy saucepan, combine sugar and cream of tartar; mix well and add water.
2. Bring to a boil, stirring constantly, and continue cooking until mixture becomes amber in color; immediately add pecans and stir.
3. Quickly spread out on a buttered cookie sheet and cool.
4. Break apart to serve.

PECAN ROLL

1 cup of sugar
1 can of sweetened condensed milk
2 tablespoons of butter
1 teaspoon of vanilla
4 cups of chopped pecans

1. Melt sugar in a teflon-coated skillet until light brown, stirring with a wooden spoon; as soon as sugar is melted, remove from the heat and add condensed milk.
2. Mix well and return to heat; continue to cook until a drop of mixture forms a soft ball in cold water, about 15 minutes.
3. Add butter, vanilla and pecans; shape into an 8- to 9-inch roll with buttered hands.
4. To serve, slice into 16-18 pieces.

OEUFS A LA NEIGE
Floating Islands

3 eggs, separated
½ cup of sugar
2 cups of milk
Grated nutmeg

1. Beat egg whites until they form stiff peaks; scald milk in a 10- or 12-inch skillet.
2. Drop spoonfuls of egg whites into simmering milk and poach about 5 minutes, turning once; remove from milk with a slotted spoon and place in a large, shallow, glass serving dish; sprinkle with grated nutmeg.
3. Beat egg yolks and sugar until light and lemon-colored; add to milk in skillet and cook about five minutes, stirring constantly, until mixture thickens.
4. Pour custard over poached egg whites; serve warm or cold.
Yield: 4 to 6 servings

VANILLA ICE CREAM

2 cups of sugar
1 tablespoon of cornstarch
½ teaspoon of salt
1 dozen eggs, beaten
1½ quarts of milk, scalded
2 cups of whipping cream
1 tablespoon of vanilla

1. Add sugar, cornstarch and salt to eggs and beat until thick and lemon-colored.
2. Add egg mixture to milk, stirring constantly, and cook over medium heat until mixture thickens enough to coat the spoon; immediately remove from heat.
3. Add whipping cream and vanilla and mix well; chill.
4. Freeze in ice cream maker according to manufacturer's instructions.
Yield: 1 gallon

RIZ AU LAIT
Rice Custard

1 cup of cooked rice
½ cup of sugar
1 quart of milk
2 egg yolks, beaten
Vanilla, to taste

1. Add cooked rice and sugar to milk in a saucepan; cook, stirring constantly, on low heat until mixture is the consistency of cream. Remove the film that forms on top as it forms.
2. Add beaten egg yolks, continuing to stir, and cook about one minute; remove from heat and stir in vanilla.
3. Serve warm or cold as a dessert.

Yield: 6 to 8 servings

Note: This is a good use of leftover rice.

BAKED CUSTARD

3 eggs, beaten
¼ cup of sugar
¼ teaspoon of salt
2 cups of milk, scalded
½ teaspoon of vanilla
Grated nutmeg

1. Combine eggs, sugar and salt; add to milk and vanilla and mix well.
2. Pour into 6 custard cups and sprinkle with nutmeg.
3. Place in a 2-inch deep baking dish and add water until it reaches half-way on the custard cups; bake at 325 degrees for 30 to 40 minutes.

Yield: 6 servings

PAIN SIROTE
Syrup Bread

2 cups of sugar cane syrup
Pinch of salt
1 tablespoon of butter
1 teaspoon of vanilla
Sliced stale bread
½ cup of chopped pecans

1. Cook syrup and salt in a heavy saucepan until it boils; reduce the heat and continue to cook until a drop of syrup forms a soft ball in cold water.
2. Add butter and vanilla and beat well.
3. Dip sliced bread into this mixture and turn each slice to be sure it is well covered with the syrup; remove from the syrup mixture and set aside on a platter or wax paper.
4. When bread cools slightly, sprinkle with pecans; let bread set in a cool drafty place until syrup is crispy.

Note: This was normally prepared during the winter months on a dry day; the syrup bread was put outdoors until crispy.

POPCORN BALLS
Tac-Tac

3 cups of sugar cane syrup
Pinch of salt
1 tablespoon of butter
3 gallons of popcorn, popped

1. Put syrup and salt in a heavy saucepan and cook until a drop forms a hard ball in a cup of cold water; remove from the heat, add butter and mix.
2. Pour syrup in a small stream over the popcorn, having another person stir the popcorn.
3. Shape popcorn balls and place on a cookie sheet to dry out.

Yield: About 3 dozen

PECAN NOUGATS

3 cups of pecans, ground
1½ cups of sugar
3 egg whites, stiffly beaten

1. Blend pecans with sugar; fold into the egg whites.
2. Roll into small balls about the size of a walnut; place on a greased cookie sheet.
3. Bake at 400 degrees until lightly brown, about 15 minutes.

Roux
Rice
Lagniappe

ROUX, RICE AND LAGNIAPPE

"First you make a roux . . ." This is the classic beginning of Cajun gumbos, fricassees, stews, bisques and many other dishes. The following procedures should be used in all recipes in this book that include a roux.

ROUX

½ cup of oil (shortening, lard, or oleo can be used)
½ cup of all-purpose flour

Heat oil in a heavy skillet (black cast-iron is normally used) over medium heat; add flour, stirring constantly. Continue to stir and cook until roux begins to lightly brown; lower heat and continue cooking and stirring until roux is of the desired degree of doneness. The entire process of making a roux can take from 30 minutes to one hour to make.

If the recipe calls for a "light brown" roux, the roux will be the color of peanut butter; if the recipe calls for a "dark brown" roux, it will be the color of chocolate. Be very careful not to burn the roux; this causes a very bitter taste in the finished recipe.

Cooked roux can be kept indefinitely in a covered jar and is used in recipes in this book calling for "prepared roux." The oil will separate in storage; simply stir it back into the roux to use.

RICE

1 cup of rice
2 cups of water
1 teaspoon of salt
1 tablespoon of butter or oil

1. Combine all ingredients in a heavy saucepan.
2. Bring to a boil, reduce heat to low, cover with a tight-fitting lid and cook 15 minutes.
3. Remove from heat and keep covered for 10 minutes.

Yield: 3 cups of cooked rice

FIG PRESERVES

15 quarts of figs
5 pounds of sugar
1 cup of water

1. Mix all ingredients in a large pot.
2. Cook over a very low heat for 3½ to 4 hours.
3. Remove fruit carefully. Pack in hot containers. Fill with boiling hot syrup and immediately process containers of all sizes 10 minutes in boiling water bath.

Yield: 12 pints

BLACKBERRY PRESERVES

1½ quarts of fresh blackberries
½ cup of water
4 cups of sugar

1. Wash and drain blackberries; combine blackberries with water and sugar in a heavy pot.
2. Bring to a boil and stir until the sugar dissolves; lower heat to medium and continue to cook until the temperature reaches 220 degrees on a candy thermometer.
3. Skim any foam off the top that may have accumulated and pour into canning jars; process for canning according to recommended procedures.

Yield: 2 to 3 pints

Index

Index